STEALING

LITTLE

MOON

STEALING
LITTLE
MOON

The Legacy of the
American Indian
Boarding Schools

DAN SASUWEH JONES

SCHOLASTIC
FOCUS
New York

Library of Congress Cataloging-in-Publication Data

Names: Jones, Dan C., 1951– author.
Title: Stealing Little Moon : the legacy of the American Indian boarding schools /
Dan SaSuWeh Jones.
Description: First edition. | New York : Scholastic Focus, 2024. | Includes bibliographical
references. | Audience: Ages 8 and up | Audience: Grades 4–6 | Summary: "Little Moon There
Are No Stars Tonight was four years old when armed federal agents showed up at her home
and took her from her family. Under the authority of the government, she was sent away to a
boarding school specifically created to strip her of her Ponca culture and teach her the ways
of white society. Little Moon was one of thousands of Indigenous children forced to attend
these schools across America and give up everything they'd ever known: family, friends, toys,
clothing, food, customs, even their language. She would be the first of four generations of
her family who would go to the Chilocco Indian Agricultural School. Dan SaSuWeh Jones
chronicles his family's time at Chilocco—starting with his grandmother Little Moon's arrival
when the school first opened and ending with him working on the maintenance crew when
the school shut down nearly one hundred years later. Together with the voices of students from
other schools, both those who died and those who survived, Dan brings to light the lasting
legacy of the boarding school era. Part American history, part family history, Stealing Little
Moon is a powerful look at the miseducation and the mistreatment of Indigenous kids,
while celebrating their strength, resiliency, and courage—and the ultimate failure of the
United States government to erase them."—provided by publisher.
Identifiers: LCCN 2024003743 (print) | LCCN 2024003744 (ebook) |
ISBN 9781338889475 (hardcover) | ISBN 9781338889499 (ebook)
Subjects: LCSH: Chilocco Indian Agricultural School—History—Juvenile literature. |
Off-reservation boarding schools—United States—History—Juvenile literature. | Indians of
North America—Cultural assimilation—History—Juvenile literature. | BISAC: JUVENILE
NONFICTION / Biography & Autobiography / Cultural, Ethnic & Regional | JUVENILE
NONFICTION / History / United States / General
Classification: LCC E97.5 .J66 2024 (print) | LCC E97.5 (ebook) |
DDC 371.829/97—dc23/eng/20240214

Printed in Italy 183
First edition, September 2024

Book design by Maeve Norton

To the four women whose stories made this book possible: Elizabeth Little Cook Pensoneau Hernandez (Little Moon There Are No Stars Tonight), Velma Louise Pensoneau Jones (Full Moon), Donna Colleen Jones Flood (Heal with Water), and Denise Michele Jones Ponds (Little Moon There Are No Stars Tonight, after her great-grandmother). For the lives you've led, the incredible hardships you've endured, and the wisdom you've passed down to all your children.

TABLE OF CONTENTS

Foreword by Denise K. Lajimodiere   ix

Introduction   xiii

Chapter One: Kill the Indian in Him: A History   1

Chapter Two: Little Moon There Are No Stars Tonight   16

Chapter Three: Little Moon at Chilocco   39

Chapter Four: Full Moon   61

Chapter Five: Athletes & Soldiers: The Warrior Spirit   85

Chapter Six: Hateful Things   111

Chapter Seven: Changes in the 1950s   139

Chapter Eight: It's OK to Be an Indian!   169

Chapter Nine: Red Power Continues   186

Chapter Ten: Chilocco Closes   205

Chapter Eleven: My Chilocco Story   218

Chapter Twelve: Let the Truth-Telling Begin   242

Conclusion   262

Bibliography   265

Photo Credits   278

Acknowledgments   279

About the Author   284

FOREWORD

In these pages, Dan SaSuWeh Jones will tell you a story about his family. It is not just any family story. It covers four generations of an American Indian family of the Ponca Nation in Oklahoma. They lived through an era that many of you never knew existed called the boarding school era. This era lasted about one hundred years, from 1869 through the 1960s, but its impact would last long after. During that time, United States government agents took young Indian children from their families and sent them to boarding schools far away. The children were forced to abandon their Native heritage and to take up the ways of white people. They were punished if they refused.

The boarding school era is one of harsh reality, horror, and sorrow. Tragically, the consequences of this era continue to affect thousands of American Indians today. I know this because I am the daughter of boarding school survivors. I grew up in a family in which both my parents and grandparents were sent to boarding schools. It took me many years to understand why my parents parented my siblings and me the way they did. We were never hugged or told "I love you." We were disciplined the way my parents were while at boarding school, with verbal abuse and often by the belt. Over the years, I had heard my parents mention being sent to boarding schools, but I never connected their discipline style toward us with their school experiences.

Later, as a teacher, I decided to record my parents' boarding school stories. My father had attended Chemawa Indian School in Oregon, while my mother had gone to Stephan Mission School in South Dakota and to Wahpeton Indian School in North Dakota. My parents spoke of emotional cruelty, hunger, physical and spiritual abuse, and extreme loneliness. I learned that when they were very young, they were made to leave their own parents and the homes they loved. They had to live full time at a school where they had few clothes and little food. They were commanded to march everywhere as if they were little soldiers. The teachers were strict and often had short tempers. The students were punished for doing things such as asking for more food to eat. Or being late for dinner. Or even speaking a few words of their own language.

After listening to my parents, I came to understand. My brothers and sisters and I were disciplined the way *they* were disciplined while at boarding school. That meant being hit with a belt, being ordered to kneel in corners, and being verbally abused. Those teachers were the only parents my mother and father knew. I believe my parents did the best they could, considering the trauma they had experienced.

When I became a college professor at the University of North Dakota, I continued my quest to learn more about what happened to students like my parents who attended boarding schools. Soon I found myself traveling throughout North and South Dakota and Minnesota, recording the stories of former students who attended such schools from the 1920s to the 1970s. I learned that most of them had been subjected to the same cruel treatment my parents and grandparents had experienced. For that reason, today they are no longer called former boarding school students. They are called boarding school survivors.

I spent the next ten years interviewing survivors, listening closely to their stories as their voices broke, their eyes welled with tears, and their hands shook with frustration and anger at their memories. I often had to take long breaks because it was such emotionally draining work. Their stories are documented in my book *Stringing Rosaries*.

During my time as a professor, there came a call from national Native American leaders. They asked for anyone who was already working to heal or help others heal from boarding school trauma to form a new organization, named the National Native American Boarding School Healing Coalition (NABS). The organization was formed in 2011. I am honored to be one of the original founding members and past board president. NABS is a Native-led coalition. Its members give support to survivors and descendants of Native American boarding schools. The coalition is an organization of about 800 individuals. For more than a decade we have used our combined voice to educate others about the truth of the federal Indian boarding school policy and the devastating consequences of that time period.

That education continues in the book you are about to read. *Stealing Little Moon* by Dan SaSuWeh Jones, is a story unlike any other I have read during my years of research and writing about boarding schools. In it, you will discover the story of a family that survived not one generation of boarding school experiences but four. The stories are sad, insightful, and compelling. They are infuriating. Sometimes they are hopeful. Those experiences began with Dan's own grandmother, Elizabeth, in the year 1885. She was just four years old. I wept for little Elizabeth and the other tiny children as they were pulled from their parents' arms. I cheered for their courage and their determination to live. Finally, I witnessed the strength of human spirit that endures in the families of boarding school survivors. That spirit allows them to speak out today, and to heal.

—Denise K. Lajimodiere,
Turtle Mountain Band,
Chippewa (Ojibwe)

Cofounder, National Native American
Boarding School Healing Coalition

Poet Laureate of North Dakota

INTRODUCTION

In 1884, Takare of the Wichita Indian Tribe of Oklahoma was the first child to die at Chilocco Indian Agricultural School, a place that would become intricately tied to my family. It was a defining moment in a place that was already building a painful and complicated history. Takare was stolen at a very young age from her parents and people by the United States government and sent to Chilocco in north-central Oklahoma, then part of the Indian Territory. There, she was called Take Care, a bitter irony given her tragic fate. The US government had established Chilocco and other boarding schools in order to force young Indian children to abandon their heritage. Officials believed that, gradually, American Indian cultures would die out. There would be no more Indian wars, no different beliefs. Everyone on the American continent would be the same.

Many other young children would share Takare's fate in the years to come, both at Chilocco and at other boarding schools across America. This is their story. These children symbolize centuries of grave mistreatment of American Indians and their culture by white colonizers who invaded our continent. From the beginning of time, we have known our land as Turtle Island. The colonizers later named the continent "America."

To all the children of Turtle Island who were mistreated, we owe a debt. It is our duty to acknowledge their stories and engrave them in our memories. It is my commitment and labor of love to bring these stories to you, because it honors the children, their families, and their heritage. And because the stories are personal to me.

I am the third generation of my immediate family to attend and work for the Chilocco Indian Agricultural School, which opened in 1884.

From its first classes to its last one in 1980, it operated for almost one hundred years to the day. During much of that time, my family attended the school. My grandmother was in its earliest classes, then came my mother and her siblings, my brother and sisters, and finally one of my nieces attended the last year the school was open. While I did not attend the school myself, I worked there at different times throughout my life, first in maintenance and then as a security guard who lived at the school after it was closed.

Throughout this book, I share the stories of my family and of others to explore the bigger story of the Indian boarding schools. As you read, think about your own first days at preschool or kindergarten. You probably couldn't wait to go home after school to be with your family. But for thousands of American Indian children who were stolen from their parents, they could not go home in the afternoon. Some never went home again. At the school, each day was long and hard. Disciplinarians ordered the children to rise early; to march everywhere they went; to eat scanty, insect-infested food; and to cook and clean. Students were severely punished if they spoke their native language or practiced their beloved cultural rituals.

In the early period, from 1884 to 1935, a single boarding school might house several hundred children. If a child like Takare died while at the school, the body might not be sent home. There was no way to preserve a body, and many families lived too far away for it to be delivered. In fact, many parents never even knew of their child's death. Today, if you were to walk the grounds of an abandoned boarding school, you would likely find a cemetery filled with unmarked graves. Such cemeteries have become sacred places to American Indians. Generally, the nearest tribes will try to care for them, but the cost of upkeep is great. It has been our request that the US government take responsibility for the care of Native American burial grounds. As you read this book, you will see why.

Culture makes us who we are. It is something humans have been exchanging since the world began. The beauty of culture is how we all do the same things in a different way, and how we learn from one another. Italian food without tomatoes from the Americas and spices from India would not be the Italian food we know today! That's just one example of how the exchange of culture influences us and makes our lives more interesting.

Arts, dance, and religion are other examples. Our different practices and beliefs impact each of us in deep and spiritual ways, and we must respect that. We learn from one another, and we are better for it. The consequences of disrespecting and diminishing other cultures are horrific.

To intentionally destroy another culture is also to remove a greater opportunity to live in a healthier world. Take, for example, the American Indians' relationship with Nature. We believe we are inseparable from our surroundings. For two hundred years, white leaders in the United States considered the natural world as something to take *from*. They overlooked the consequences. Eventually, America used up or destroyed its valuable resources, leaving future generations without. Finally, the government had to start passing laws to stop people and industry from wasteful and destructive practices. In many cases, it was too late and too little. Today, slowly, the American outlook is shifting toward this ancient American Indian belief: Take only what you can replace. Hold a spiritual connection with Nature as its caretaker. If the white leaders of the new United States had listened to the people who had cared for the land for thousands of years, they might have recognized the value of those cultural beliefs. We might live in a stronger, healthier, and more self-sufficient nation today.

Despite the deep and troubling nature of this topic, I have taken on the challenge of writing about it because it is a story that must be told and heard. History books and classes will not teach students about the boarding school era, even though it existed for over a hundred years, well into recent times. Why do we know so little about this era? Perhaps because it brought so much loss to societies both American Indian and white. This network of government schools was designed to wipe out American Indian culture and replace it with white ways. While Indian cultures ultimately survived, they suffered damage, beginning with individuals. Forced to leave their families to attend the schools, children had to disown their language and rituals, and they were brainwashed into adopting white ways. Whether or not they "obeyed" the rules, the children were abused emotionally and physically by the administrators and teachers. After they returned home and married, many passed on this abuse to the next generations. During the era and continuing today, dedicated tribal members have worked to heal our people and reinstill our ways in new generations. Thanks to these leaders, our strong and ancient cultural connections, and our deep-rooted spiritual beliefs, we have survived. And once again we are thriving.

In this book you will experience the anguish faced long ago by other young people your age. Imagine their world. They were forced to abandon their native language for English. They had to follow Christian practices that had nothing to do with their own spirituality. Many generations of American Indians suffered these and other abuses that brought devastating consequences to our cultures.

I will tell their stories and those of my own family members. As you read, you can draw your own conclusions. You'll meet my grandmother Elizabeth; my mother, Velma; her brother Edward; her half sister, Otilia; and her half brothers Francis and Daniel; my sisters Donna and Esther; my older brother, Mike; my first cousin, whom I call sister, Charmain; and my niece Denise. There were others, too, like my first cousins and sisters Betty and Darlene, who experienced Chilocco. In the end, they certainly all survived. They also thrived.

Eventually, even the government had to face the reality of its actions. By the late 1920s, ongoing reports of abuse and deplorable conditions had leaked out from the schools to government ears. Such news prompted a deep government investigation. The resulting Meriam Report came out in 1928 and exposed unspeakable conditions. It also made three recommendations: to abolish courses that taught only European American values; to keep young children at home, in local day schools; and, within communities, to give American Indians the education and skills they needed to live. By 1935, the youngest children were going home. Schools were losing attendance. Some closed. Sadly, many stayed open. European American values remained in place. Students still learned to be white. Abuse continued.

Still, the Meriam Report had opened a new era of awareness.

Indian communities celebrated their cultures and held on to them more tightly. They watched and waited. By the 1950s, students and leaders of Indian Nations began to push back. They demanded that the schools allow them to speak their languages and celebrate their heritage. They spoke out at rallies and protests to inform the American public of the horrors many students experienced. They stood steadfast in their pride. Finally, some schools started to introduce American Indian culture into their curriculum. There were language classes or pageants in which students wore tribal dress and performed traditional dances. Later, schools allowed the male students to grow their hair long again, a cultural and spiritual custom.

This book honors Takare and every child who followed her. It explores what it was like to be an American Indian child during the boarding school years, from 1884 to 1980, as well as the depth and richness of our heritage. Its cultures and beliefs are so complex that white society could not understand them enough to cherish them. This is a story of sadness. But it is also a story of hope. Above all, it is a story of the amazing resilience of the human spirit.

CHAPTER ONE

Kill the Indian in Him: A History

All residential boarding schools were created with the same intention: to forcibly assimilate, or integrate, American Indian children into white European culture. Many schools treated students with extreme cruelty. Others had better reputations. The Chilocco Indian Agricultural School in Oklahoma that my family attended was a Quaker school. For the most part, its students reported good experiences. Still, the teachers were stern, and rules were rules that everyone had to follow. Chilocco, along with Haskell Institute in Kansas, are the only schools I know of out of over four hundred that have active alumni groups today. I see that as a sign that many students made lasting friendships at both institutions, and they still hold reunions where they tell stories and laugh. This is far different from the experiences children had at many other schools.

The history of the earliest American Indian schools begins four hundred years ago with mission schools. They were established by Spanish colonizers along the West Coast of North America in the early 1600s. Not long after, in the northeastern

United States, British colonizers established Harvard University in 1636 to train Puritan ministers. Then, in 1655, they added the Indian College to bring Christianity to the surrounding Native people. The idea was that Indian students would live at the college, go to lectures, and dine with English students. Then they would return to their tribes to spread their new knowledge and Christian teachings. Only a handful of Indians attended the college before it was torn down in 1698. But Harvard had set the stage for future American Indian boarding schools. Those schools would be constructed by the US government and often turned over to religious groups to administer. The schools' duties would be the same: to teach white ways to Indian students, including converting them to Christianity. Some two hundred years of isolated efforts to educate and convert Indians would pass before such a system was established.

After 1865 and the end of the US Civil War, many people wanted to start new lives in new places. They immediately looked toward the American West. The lands they wanted to "settle" had already belonged to American Indians for thousands of years, and these original people did not plan to part with their homelands. Not only did the lands have deep ancestral and spiritual meanings, but they were rich with natural resources, including buffalo and other wildlife that provided food, clothing, and shelter. The Indians fought the white intruders, and the ongoing conflict became known to the government as "the Indian Problem." Eventually, the stronger US forces prevailed. Starting in the late 1870s, the government began taking away tens of millions of acres of Indian lands to sell to white settlers. Tribes were forcibly removed from their ancestral homes and relocated to small government reservations. Still, American Indians pushed back. Skirmishes continued throughout the West.

During this time, a US Army captain, Richard Henry Pratt, began an experiment. Pratt had served in the Civil War, then later in the Indian Wars on the Western Frontier. In 1875, he was ordered to bring captured American Indian warriors from the West to be exiled at Fort Marion, Florida. Once the prisoners arrived, Pratt was assigned to work with them. He determined that by reeducating the warriors to white ways, he could make them contributing members of white society. He gradually developed a program that compelled the prisoners to learn the language, wear the clothing, and practice the customs of white people. The warriors were trained to work in jobs such as picking oranges or operating sawmill equipment. This process was called forced assimilation. The warriors were supported by the white community and soon lived in modest houses and worked at low-wage jobs. Their warrior spirit seemed to be taken out of them. The US government deemed the program a success.

Richard Henry Pratt.

Pratt later flaunted his pride. Speaking to a group of Baptist ministers, he compared his plan to a kind of religious baptism. The best way to civilize Indians, he said, was to "immerse" them in white society and keep them there "until thoroughly soaked."

Then Pratt had another idea. Since the assimilation program seemed so successful for adults, he thought it could be even more successful for children. Children would be less resistant to new rules. Children would more easily adapt to a new lifestyle. Children would carry traditions that were white instead of Indian, and they would pass those traditions to new generations. Pratt determined that government boarding schools could

4

train young children to do all this. They would grow up speaking the white language, practicing white culture, and following white rules. Pratt theorized that if both whites and Indians had the same kind of background and outlook, people would live peacefully. The "Indian Problem" would be solved.

Why didn't the government simply send enough troops to destroy the Indian populations? Once the tribes were cornered on reservations, it would have been relatively easy for the soldiers to carry out such a genocide. Government leaders thought about this. They decided it was more humane to carry out "cultural" genocide, or reeducation to white ways. It was also a matter of expense. The US Secretary of the Interior Carl Schurz calculated that the cost to kill a single Indian warrior in battle would be about one million dollars. To educate one child over an eight-year period, then send them back to their tribe to help reeducate others or to blend in to the white world, would cost only $1,200.

In 1879, Pratt opened Carlisle Indian Industrial School, the first off-reservation federal boarding school. It would be run like Fort Marion, only with children. Young students would be forced to learn white ways from their earliest years. Pratt would later state his motto, "Kill the Indian in him, and save the man." He convinced Congress that by stripping Indian children of their heritage and cultural practices, he could turn them into "civilized" citizens who could live among the "best classes" of white Americans. They would become part of white society. Gradually, Indian society would die out.

Did anyone ask our people what we felt? After all the loss and trauma our Elders had experienced throughout the nineteenth century, they could not believe that now the white men would take their children, too. As author David Wallace Adams wrote in his book *Education for Extinction*, "the white man had concluded that the only way to save Indians was to [culturally] destroy them, that the last great Indian war should be waged against the children. They were coming for the children."

And come they did. Government agents entered reservations in North and South Dakota to take the first group of children, 120 in all, to Carlisle. The school was established on the grounds of an old military base outside Carlisle, Pennsylvania. It had once housed Revolutionary War soldiers and later Civil War soldiers. The government had chosen this site partly because it was on a railroad line and convenient for transporting children across the country. They wanted a school that was hundreds, even thousands, of miles from the western Indian reservations. By separating the students from their families and traditions, the children would more easily adopt white culture. Officials also wanted a place close enough to Washington, DC, so that they could visit frequently to monitor the school's progress.

The first students arrived at the school at midnight on October 6, 1879. They had journeyed some 1,500 miles from the

Student body assembled on the Carlisle School grounds.

Rosebud and Pine Ridge Reservations in South Dakota, traveling first by horse, then steamboat, and finally by train. Their arrival was planned for the middle of the night so that local residents would not come out to gawk. But even in the darkness, a crowd waited. These were the first of more than ten thousand young American Indians who would pass through Carlisle over the next forty years. They would come from 142 tribes across the nation, including Sioux, Cherokee, Chippewa, and Alaska Natives.

Luther Standing Bear, of the Lakota tribe, was in this first arriving class. He later wrote of his apprehension: "I could think of no reason why white people wanted Indian boys and girls, except to kill them . . . I thought we were going East to die. But so well had courage and bravery been trained into us . . . in going East I was proving to my father that he was honored with a brave son." Along the way, he and other boys sang brave songs so they could meet death "according to the Lakota code—fearlessly." Luther survived and adapted to the white world.

Run like a military institution, Carlisle required the Indian students to cut their long braids, to take "American" names, to dress in drab US military uniforms, to speak only English, and to march wherever they went around campus as if they were little soldiers. Each student was even assigned a military ranking. For the children, the act of being ripped from their families had been traumatizing. Now these new rules added distress to their overwhelming grief. And each new rule isolated the children more and more from the culture and families that had taught them the basic concepts of respect, generosity, and love.

Imagine being told how to act and what to believe by a people who have moved you from your land to a faraway place. Their beliefs, actions, and morals do not resemble yours at all. But you are told that their outlooks and ways of life are better. They are the only ones that work. You might be surprised that both American Indians and white Americans shared the golden rule, "Do unto others as you would want them to do unto you." But the rule seemed to mean different things to each people. Indians shared their lands and helped white men's culture flourish. White men took the land for their own and attempted to erase American Indian cultures. Now the children had to suffer the consequences of the Indians' generosity.

The immediate changes in the students' appearances would have shocked their Elders. These were recorded in before-and-after photographs. Young Hastiin To'Haali, of the Navajo, or Diné, Nation, attended Carlisle from 1882 to 1886. His "before" photograph shows a young man with flowing hair, who is elegant in full Native dress. His "after" picture is of a boy with a shorn head, in a drab military uniform. In both pictures, his eyes brim with sadness. After Hastiin To'Haali and the other students were made to change their outward appearance, they were given a pointer and told to point to a blackboard scribbled with American names. The one they chose was then hung around their neck. Hastiin To'Haali chose "Tom." His last name would become "Torlino," a misspelling of his Navajo name. When he left Carlisle in 1886 and returned to his home in Coyote Canyon, New Mexico, Tom took up his family's long-standing work in ranching. He used his education to help others in the Navajo tribe communicate with the white community. But he never again regained his full status as an Indian. He was called Hastiin Bilagáana (meaning "white person" in Navajo) for the rest of his life.

Luther Standing Bear as a child (top)
and after arriving at Carlisle (bottom).

Hastiin To'Haali as he entered Carlisle in 1882 (top)
and Tom Torlino as he was known in 1885 (bottom).

In the eyes of Pratt and other administrators, students like Luther and Tom were success stories. They excelled in English language, writing, music, the arts, and sports. Pratt made sure that the officials in Washington saw this. He invited them to Carlisle to attend student band concerts and sports events. He established a school newspaper for white supporters to read. In it, students reported on their excellent experiences at Carlisle, whether they were true or not. Pratt even turned a classroom into a photography lab to document his so-called success in pictures. Not only did he take before-and-after photographs of every student, but he ensured that photographs documented classroom experiences, concerts, sports, and happy interactions with the staff. Pratt easily sold Congress on a project to open similar schools throughout America. Carlisle would become the model for more than four hundred other boarding schools.

The second off-reservation boarding school in the United States, Chemawa Indian School, was founded just a year later, in 1880, on the West Coast. That school was run by Pratt's former colleague at Fort Marion, Lieutenant Melville Wilkinson. First situated in Forest Grove, Oregon, the school was moved a few miles south to Salem, where it stands today. Children from nearby tribes, mainly the Puyallup Indians of Washington's Puget Sound, were not only the first enrolled, but they also built the school. Later students came from as far away as New Mexico, Arizona, and Alaska. Chemawa, like Carlisle, trained

Chemawa Indian School students in their
military-inspired uniforms.

students as if they were in military boot camp—it was "run by
the bell." Gradually, the young Indians' culture, language, and
family ties faded.

Soon, military-minded schools sprang up across the nation
modeled after Carlisle and Chemawa. By 1885, schools included
Haskell in Kansas, Albuquerque Indian School in New Mexico,
and Genoa Indian School in Nebraska. In the 1890s, more
schools would open their doors in Phoenix, Arizona; Sherman,
California; and Flandreau, South Dakota. Enrollment began

immediately. Government Indian agents would tour the homes of nearby Indian reservations and forcibly take children from their families to live at the schools. If families refused, there would be penalties. Tabatha Toney Booth, of the University of Central Oklahoma, wrote in her research paper *Cheaper Than Bullets*, "Many parents had no choice but to send their kids, when Congress authorized the Commissioner of Indian Affairs to withhold rations, clothing, and annuities of those families that refused to send students . . . Sometimes resistant fathers found themselves locked up for refusal. In 1895, nineteen men of the Hopi Nation were imprisoned to Alcatraz because they refused to send their children to boarding school." American Indian communities tried to save their children. Parents taught them to hide when agents came near. Native police refused to help the kidnapping agents. Still, the United States government was stronger.

This new system of schools complemented the long-existing mission schools that had been started by Christians, Unitarians, and other religious sects. But they all worked toward the same goal. Whether government- or church-run, they all wanted to "civilize" the Native people, meaning to make them like the white man.

The school that would educate my own family members was established in 1882. Government officials wanted a grand agricultural school in Indian Territory, today known as the state of Oklahoma. More than 8,000 acres of land that had once belonged to the Cherokee reservation was set aside by the government to fulfill this vision. Officials wanted the school to be close to Kansas so it could serve both the Ponca and Pawnee reservations. When they assigned Major James Haworth as the superintendent, he pushed back. Weren't the schools supposed to be far away from reservations so that students wouldn't be tempted to run away and return home? Or so their parents wouldn't want to visit constantly? But the government insisted.

Haworth searched for the perfect building site. At last, on the banks of Chilocco Creek, on the remotest possible piece of land, in the middle of empty, tall-grass prairie, he found it. Soon limestone dug from local quarries and hauled to the site was lifted into a structure that towered three-and-a-half stories above the prairie. Steps led eight feet up to a massive porch. The school held classrooms and dormitories for 150 students. There was an enormous kitchen, dining rooms, and staff dorms. The only building for miles around, Chilocco's lights shone like a beacon across the prairie at sunset. It was ready.

In late January 1884, several wagons holding 100 children from Cheyenne, Arapaho, Kiowa, and Comanche tribes drew up to the entrance. Soon they would be followed by children from the Ponca and other nations. The Chilocco story had begun.

CHAPTER TWO

Little Moon There Are No Stars Tonight

My grandmother's family, the Little Cooks, made the most of a life that had been imposed upon them by the US government. In 1877, the government had pushed the Ponca tribe out of their ancestral homeland in today's Nebraska and onto a reservation in what is now Oklahoma. It was unfriendly land. The soil was acidic, the waters scarce. Miles from their beloved lands rich with natural beauty and fertile soil, the Little Cooks worked hard for their basic survival.

By 1880, they had built a small farm. Life there was very slow. They lived by the seasons, eating foods that were either home-grown or harvested from nature. In springtime, wild potatoes, mushrooms, onions, arrowroot, and cattail root grew abundantly. The men and boys went fishing and hunting for small game. The women and girls planted gardens. In late summer and fall, they harvested fruits and vegetables to preserve for the cold winter months ahead. The family raised a few cattle for meat, as most Indians do not drink milk. They had chickens and pigs. The women and girls washed laundry and mended clothing. Clothes had to last. Buying new clothes was not something they did often. Their home had no electricity or plumbing. Later in her life, my grandmother recalled that, as a young child, she was potty trained in an outhouse, or in a pot indoors when the weather turned cold.

In the early 1880s, my grandmother was too young to help around the house. But she followed her older sisters around and tried to do what they did. They took turns playing with her, and often. Her toys were mostly handmade, but once in a while she was given a store-bought toy or dress. The family didn't go to town very often, but when they did, it was like going into the future. There were so many new inventions. Even to see an automobile was very special.

The Little Cooks owned a wagon. If they wanted to visit family or friends, they would have to travel for one or two days because houses were so far apart. It meant fording rivers across shallow areas or taking a ferry when the water was deep. For a couple pennies per person and a nickel a wagon, they could board a small barge. Then a man on the other side would pull it across by a rope. When the visitors finally arrived at the other family's home, they would stay a week or several weeks. They brought tents to camp in, and they happily joined in the work. The men built new structures. The women sewed beautiful quilts out of small scraps of material. They cooked and worked in the garden. The children played together.

With their family and friends, the Little Cooks built a tight-knit unit. In their homes, they carried on their Ponca customs and values. They spoke and sang their musical language, they told ancient stories, they danced, and they laughed. The French who first met the Ponca in the 1700s called us "a very strong people, who deeply love their children." That would have been true in my grandmother's time as well.

My grandmother's name in Ponca when translated into English was Little Moon There Are No Stars Tonight. Her American name was Elizabeth Little Cook. In 1885, Elizabeth was just four years old when the Indian agent came to her parents' rural home, in a wagon half-full of other Ponca Indian children. On a mission as serious as this one, removing a child from their home, he would travel with an entourage of several wagons driven by mule skinners (drivers). Next to each skinner sat a guard armed with a shotgun. There might be a detail of soldiers traveling slightly behind the agent's entourage. They would be close enough to quickly respond to any trouble.

Just their presence had the intended results. The agent meant business, and he had both the manpower and the federal government to back up his authority on the Ponca Tribal Reserve, in the present-day states of Oklahoma, Kansas, Nebraska, and part of Iowa. This time of the year, in the fall, the night fog would always be gone soon after the sun rose. But not this morning. It felt different, the air was unusually heavy with moisture, and someone menacing was out there.

Elizabeth's father, my great-grandfather Sam Little Cook, was not a tall man, but he was strong and stockily built. He was a Chief of our people and the Head Chief of our clan, sometimes called the Rain Band. In his traditional regalia he wore a full war bonnet made of golden eagle feathers. It ran from his head to the ground. Few other men had the standing to wear this special headdress. Now, with intruders nearby, Sam could read the signs as well or better than most. He could smell the wet horses and the reek of men who rarely bathed. He could tell by how quiet they kept their horses that they were trained warriors. Even the horses were trained as warriors, instinctively knowing the signs of impending conflict. These unseen men could be only one thing: a partial platoon of the US Cavalry.

Sam kept a rifle over the front door, but in this case, he knew its use would be fruitless and maybe a big mistake. With quiet urgency he told his wife, my great-grandmother Esther Broken Jaw Little Cook, to hide their six children, ages four to eighteen: daughters Creth, Annie, Fannie, and Elizabeth, and older sons David and Henry. Sam silently went about his early morning ritual chopping wood for the cookstove, all the time listening intently. While Sam was piling armfuls of chopped wood on his porch, he noticed a horse-drawn surrey approaching from the same direction where the unseen horsemen hovered. Behind the surrey was a wagon loaded with children. Ponca children. Sam recognized some of the kids as belonging to his neighbors and kinfolk.

In the surrey he recognized the Indian agent named Whiteman. The man next to him was a Ponca interpreter. The wagon was being driven by a large, burly man, and sitting on the rickety seats were several white women, some holding the smaller children. Sam had no idea what this was all about, but he was concerned. And there were still those soldiers down among the trees, out of sight. Sam threw his last load of firewood on the porch and stood tall, watching as the party halted and waiting for the agent to speak. From the buckboard the agent called out to my great-grandfather in English: "We have come after Elizabeth. It's time for her to begin school." The interpreter translated his words, and Sam responded in Ponca: "She is just a baby. She needs to be with her mother!"

"Sam," the agent continued, "we don't want trouble, but the girl has to come with us!"

Esther, listening behind the door, could not believe what she was hearing. They had come to take her baby. The family had already been through so much. First there was the nightmare of being forced by the government to leave their homes and relocate in Indian Territory. Now there was this. What kind of monsters were these invaders?

THE PONCA TRAIL OF TEARS

By the time little Elizabeth was taken from them, Sam and Esther Little Cook had already suffered deeply at the hands of white Americans. So had their entire Ponca Nation. For centuries, the Ponca had lived in today's Nebraska, on lush farmland along the Niobrara River. When white men came west in the 1800s, the Ponca signed many peaceful treaties with the US government. They traded. The Ponca gave land to white settlers.

However, during the 1860s, Ponca enemies, the Sioux, threatened both the Ponca and white settlers. To keep peace, the US government gave Ponca land to the Sioux. Then, without any warning, in 1877, US soldiers forced the Ponca to move. They had to walk 600 miles south, to today's Oklahoma, then called Indian Territory. Sam and Esther Little Cook joined their people. It was springtime. Heavy rains flooded the roads. Bridges washed out. For two months they walked. They suffered during cold nights. On hot days as the sun beat down, insects swarmed around them. Many fell ill. A tornado struck their camp.

Elders and children died and were buried along the rocky trail, far from their ancestral home. The new land was barren and unfit for farming.

The Little Cooks and others refused to stay. But government agents held them prisoner, warning they would be punished if they tried to leave. The families survived, scratching out a living. Sam and Esther could not know that one day they would suffer a greater trial.

The women who had come with the wagon had seen the older sisters whisk away Elizabeth and hide her in one of the outbuildings. A few of them climbed down and hurried to find the girls. One grabbed Elizabeth and dragged her to the wagon as she kicked and screamed. Her sisters ran to help her, but the other women held them back. Elizabeth was forced into the wagon before her mother knew what was happening. When Esther came to the porch amid her family's screams and shouts and saw that they had her baby daughter, she was overcome with fear and anger. As she ran to pull Elizabeth from the wagon, she was restrained by the agents' assistants. Sam started to race to help his wife, then he stopped. He was aware one of the men was holding a shotgun. Sam and other members of his family might

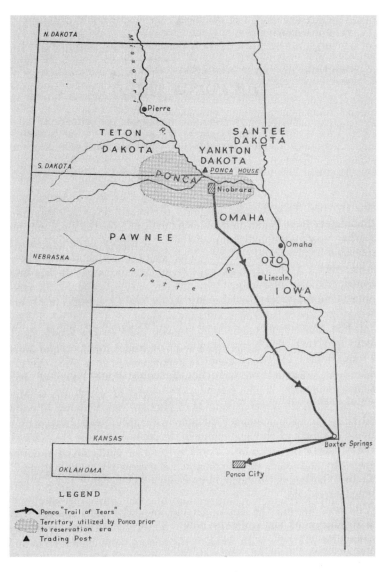

Map of the Ponca Trail of Tears.

be shot if he pulled Elizabeth from the wagon. There were other punishments as well. Local agents could withhold government food allotments and put his family on a watch list. The reservation land was not fertile enough to grow crops to feed them, and they needed the government food rations each month. Standing up to government agents meant being tagged as "rebellious" and being watched closely. Any false move in the agents' eyes, and the family could lose food benefits or be harassed in other ways. Or worse. In this moment, Sam feared the situation was so intense that someone could easily be shot by the gun-toting officers. Better to let her go, to save the seven remaining family members. With Esther sobbing beside him, Sam watched, powerless, as the entourage turned and disappeared into the fog.

They took Elizabeth without any of her clothes or the toys she cherished. She was stolen by force from our family at just four years old. It was so traumatic that the whole family, especially my great-grandmother Esther, never forgot or really got over it. Esther mourned for years. There was no way to recover from having her baby taken from her. For a family who had already suffered many tragic events, it is one of the crueler episodes in our family history.

For Elizabeth the nightmare was just beginning. Herded into the convoy of wagons along with other Ponca children, she was held by a matron since she was among the youngest. Sobbing as she was pulled away from her home, Elizabeth felt she was in a bad dream, moving in slow motion. Watching her disappear, her distraught parents clung to each other. Her sisters and two older brothers huddled together, helpless. These were the memories Elizabeth would carry for the rest of her life.

Late in the day, the wagon convoy slowly rolled into the small community of White Eagle, about ten miles away. It wasn't much. The wooden homes were built in semicircles, almost in the same way the Ponca had once set up their seasonal hunting encampments in winter and summer. What Elizabeth saw was not the scene from stories she had been told of generations past. These were not the semicircles of buffalo-hide tepees nestled together on the prairie, with the colorful flags of their seven clans fluttering proudly above. Instead, her eyes met a series of squat structures, dark and forbidding. This place would become a permanent community for the Ponca Nation. There was a sawmill, a trading post, and a mission for a meeting hall. Rarely used, the hall would become a storage shed for the rations promised by the government, which were always late and never sufficient for the entire community. The goods, especially cattle, were often intercepted by white businessmen in Kansas before the shipment reached the Poncas, then were used for the white man's profits.

The first cattle brought by train were unloaded in a corral where our local convenience store, Little Dance, stands today. Only twenty cattle had arrived from the government. Many, many more had been promised. Quietly, the Ponca men who had come to watch walked up, cocked their rifles, and systematically shot the cattle. Agent Whiteman was screaming for them to stop. "You are supposed to raise these cattle and grow a herd!" he cried. Our Chief White Eagle calmly took hold of Agent Whiteman's arm. "Our people are starving, and these twenty will be needed for food right now. What you need to do is bring us the number of cattle you promised us!"

ELIZABETH WOULD NEVER KNOW THIS

Elizabeth would never experience the excitement of traveling with her Ponca tribe, but she often heard stories of her seminomadic people traveling to their winter and summer villages to hunt buffalo. Seven clans made up the full tribe. At each season they would travel together, carrying the clan flags on tall poles. These flags were used to signal from one clan to another: "We have a problem here," or "We need water soon," or "We need to rest for the Elders." Young men called Runners ran between the clans, carrying word to the leaders who followed the tribe. The leaders always walked behind the people, it is said, so they would know the people's needs. The tribe would travel along rivers to sites where permanent tepee poles marked their seasonal village.

With the other children, Elizabeth would have watched the hundreds of young boys comb the woods, called timber, for squirrels, rabbits, deer, and other small game. Hunting with sticks they used like boomerangs, they would bring their catches to camp every night to fill the pots. Each season, one little girl was chosen to carry seven pipes for the seven clans. Called the Pipe Carrier, she represented the future of the entire tribe. Walking ahead of the hundreds of travelers, this child might appear lost, wandering alone on the prairie. But she was always safe. The tribe's most able warriors, called Scouts, would never let her out of their sight. She could not see the Scouts, as two rode or walked on either side of her and one ahead, but they escorted her and the entire tribe safely to the encampment.

When Elizabeth's parents were young, they had loved this life, rich in community and symbolism. It was stopped forever when white men killed most of the 200 million buffalo and moved Ponca families to reservations in the 1870s.

In the middle of White Eagle stood the school—a large three-story building. It was built by the US government in the 1880s to house the Ponca orphans who had lost their families during the Ponca Trail of Tears. Now, even children who *had* families were being rounded up and sent to White Eagle School. These children would soon be students in the boarding school program, where Ponca customs and values would be destroyed.

PONCA VALUES

Generosity has always been an important value to American Indians, something that was often misunderstood and taken advantage of by white people. While the white men took away our lands and resources, we continued giving and giving. Here is an example.

The Gives Water family is a large family within the Ponca Nation. This extended family was known as the Gives Water Society. One day in the 1890s, a family Elder was charged with going thirty miles from the reservation near today's Ponca City, Oklahoma, to Arkansas City, Kansas. The train from the east unloaded its cargo there, and it was a hub for stores and supplies going into Indian Country. Family members had put together their money so the Elder could buy six months of rations for the entire family. The Elder and his wife set off. The next day, they had nearly completed the thirty-mile wagon ride home with their full load of provisions. They passed the local Ponca cemetery and came across a young Ponca woman. They could see she was distraught and had been crying. When they stopped and asked the young woman what was wrong, she told them she had buried her husband, who died of illness. Before her husband died, the Indian agent had taken her children away to the boarding school, so she was alone and had no one. She said she didn't know how she was going to live. So, the Elder Chief and his wife climbed down from the wagon and told the young woman to take it. The old man gave the young woman the wagon, his horses, and all the provisions.

The Elder couple walked home and told the Society what they had done. No one questioned their actions, and all understood it was the right thing to do. In our culture we are taught to give until it hurts.

As Elizabeth and the other children in the convoy were unloaded and herded through White Eagle's doors, they had no idea that they were saying goodbye to who they were and all they had known. The series of events that would happen next would define Elizabeth and her traveling companions for the rest of their lives. As with the two boys Luther Standing Bear and Tom Torlino, the process of assimilation would begin immediately. It would start with the school completely altering the children's outward appearance. Each new forced change would add up to an increasingly drastic transformation, removing deep parts of Elizabeth's heritage. The idea was to make her and the other children a blank slate, then to fill the slate with white ways. To the school administrators, each step seemed simple and clean. But the meanings of a child's hair, language, and even their name were beyond the white understanding. They were sacred. At four years old, a child like Elizabeth could not explain this or defend herself against such violations.

First, Elizabeth's shining black braids were cut into a bob. To the Ponca and other tribes, a person's hair is rich in spiritual meaning. The act of braiding our hair is filled with prayer. With each braid we are communing with Wa KoN Da (God) and asking for mercy, healing, safety, clarity, and forgiveness for our infractions. We send prayers that we believe have power to heal people and all things. We ask for protection for loved ones and even our enemies, that understanding may take place through God's will and power. We pray as we braid our hair in the morning and at times throughout the day.

Metha Gives Water Collins, a Ponca grandmother to many before her passing, recalled her mother carefully braiding her hair the day she left for the white man's school: "Mother put my hair in two braids. She also made two strands of small beads strung together, and she tied eight dimes on these hair beads and tied them on my hair. The dimes jingled every time my head turned. I was overjoyed to know that this must be something special to be prepared for." Once at the school, Little Metha was stunned at breakfast when a disciplinarian strode up behind her and "jerked my hair beads off my braids in a second and flipped me backward off the bench. A scream was all that came out of me . . . From that day on I moved in fear of everyone and I couldn't trust anyone. This move made on me by Mr. Furry never did leave me. If my heart was weak, he would have killed me. What he did with my hair beads, with my eight dimes, I'll never know."

Today, as we have forever, we wear our hair with a part straight down the center of our head, to remind us that this is our path in life, honoring the path our people have followed throughout time, and to move straightforward through life. For ceremonies we may paint the part with a sacred red clay. The red paint reminds us of the blood of our relatives who have gone before us and that one day we will be reunited. To some of us, hair is a very powerful tool in our consciousness and connects us to our human spirit. We may wear a third braid on top of our heads so that, from this sacred place on the human body, our spirit may come and go. That third braid is also a tool we use when we dress in our traditional clothing. Our headdress, which symbolizes a crown of energy through which our spirit passes, is attached to that braid. To some who can see it, this energy is so powerful that it will glow.

Regardless of gender, we all have similar beliefs when it comes to cutting hair. Through time, many have believed that hair is cut only under high-stress conditions, for instance when a loved one dies. It is a symbol of mourning. Long hair that is cut then disconnects a person from the community for one year, while it grows back. White school administrators may have thought that they were only changing the children's fashion. But for Elizabeth and the children with her, having their hair cut represented death. The trauma of having her hair cut would last Elizabeth's lifetime.

The cutting of Elizabeth's hair was compounded by the school rule that she had to wear drab uniforms issued by the government. There was one kind for school and one kind for work. Thick black cotton stockings and heavy bloomers completed the uniform. A simple gray sweater was all she had to keep her warm in winter, and her moccasins were replaced with black leather shoes. Rich or poor, an American Indian child was proud of being an individual and showed it through personal dress and possessions. Tribal families have certain colors, designs, and even animals that identify them and their beliefs. For example, my grandmother's moccasins may have been embroidered with deer prints or the figures of birds—animals that represented her family clan and tribe. She and the other students became little cadets, little military soldiers who were cookie-cutter images of one another. The unique identity of American Indian dress was no longer part of each child's belief.

MY GRANDMOTHER'S MOCCASINS

The symbols embroidered on my grandmother's moccasins represented the family's connection to the sky. Our family is called the Rain Band, a subgroup of a larger Ponca clan known as Hesada, whose symbol is a sacred object, an eagle's leg dried and attached to a medicine bundle. *Hesada* means "This is the way to God." The clan never wavers from their designated path.

Through time, my ancestors have been weather forecasters and rainmakers. At birth, the women are named for objects from the sky, such as the moon, the stars, the wind, and the rain. My grandmother, Little Moon There Are No Stars Tonight, named her daughter (my mother) Full Moon. My sister Donna Jones was Heal with Water (from the sky) and my brother Mike's daughter Denise is also Little Moon There Are No Stars Tonight, same as my grandmother. My own first daughter's name is Bright Star. My second daughter, who was born during a full eclipse, is called Moon That Passes Over the Sun. As the moon continued its orbit out of the eclipse, I watched her first cry at exactly the moment the first light of the sun shot out from behind the moon. The burst was like light passing through a diamond, and so Diamond became her American name.

Light permeates the names of the women in my family. In our culture light is vision, clarity, knowledge, and spirituality. Their names are synonymous with those treasures. When Little Moon was stolen and her name changed, her light was stolen from her and from all of us.

The next violation included changing a child's name, which usually happened at the boarding school. For Elizabeth, however, the change had already taken place years earlier, at birth. After her family was abruptly moved to Indian Territory in 1877, the government demanded that all families take American names. Her name to her family would always be Little Moon There Are No Stars Tonight. To the rest of the world, it became Elizabeth.

There is cultural and historic significance in an American Indian name. For instance, at birth my great-grandmother was given the name White Buffalo Calf Robe. But she was later named Esther Broken Jaw by the white community. They believed that each person must have an American name, so they combined Esther with a male ancestor's name, Broken Jaw. Our family believes that the ancestor had been named Broken Jaw in a historic event. Perhaps he was a warrior who had his jaw severely broken while bravely fighting the enemy. Broken Jaw is a hero's name. That name was intended for him and him alone. However, white men believed everyone needed a first and last name. So they took his name and turned it into the last name for his entire family and all his descendants to come. The name Broken Jaw no longer defined only my great-grandmother's ancestral hero and the historic event he had endured. Now it was attached to her entire family, who had nothing to do with it. Instead, the family members should have had their own unique names to

Chiricahua Apache students at Carlisle before (above) and after (below).
Students in after image are (left to right): Hugh Chee, Frederick Eskelsejah,
Clement Seanilzay, Samson Noran (top row); Ernest Hogee, Margaret Y.
Nadasthilah (middle row); Humphrey Escharzay, Beatrice Kiahtel, Janette
Pahgostatum, Bishop Eatennah, and Basil Ekharden (bottom row).

identify their own personalities, experiences, and connections to the universe.

The administrators usually did not understand the reason for a specific name and would confuse the meaning, taking away its importance or impact. Sometimes they even turned it into an insult as was the case in this story from Ava Hamilton, an Arapaho filmmaker. A young man had a last name in his Arapaho language that meant "Beautiful Piercing Eyes." He had the type of eyes that could see your soul. When the agent or his assistants attempted to translate his name into English, they turned it into "Goggle Eyes"—as in big, protruding eyes. The family later dropped the word *eyes*. Today they are known as the Goggle family. I hope Eugene and his family don't mind that I passed this story down and I hope I got it right; it's important to let the world know the lasting impact the boarding schools have on our families, even now.

So, like the name of the boy with beautiful eyes, my grandmother's name and its significance were disregarded by white society. Exactly how Little Moon There Are No Stars Tonight came to be named Elizabeth, I do not know. A likely scenario is that a group of US government representatives simply decided that she looked like an Elizabeth. Or perhaps her mother, Esther, chose it because the sound of *Elizabeth* seemed more lyrical or less offensive than other American names. Or, perhaps, like

Tom Torlino, Esther and Sam simply pointed to the name *Elizabeth* on a blackboard in a US government building.

At the White Eagle School, my grandmother Elizabeth was joined mainly by students taken from other Ponca families, but there were also children from our Nez Perce neighbors to the west at Fort Oakland and Otoe-Missouria neighbors to the south. Elizabeth was not allowed to go home, but her family came to visit her often. Her eyes would light up as her three older sisters, her two older brothers, and her mother and father walked through the school doors. Elizabeth was small for her age, and in the early days her sisters made sure that the older Ponca girls watched out for her. They wanted to be sure their little sister's hair was combed and her face was washed, and that she was not hurt. The older girls put her into a lower bunk where she could see out the window at night, and it was easy for her to get in and out of bed. One night in those early, lonely days, as my grandmother peered out the window, she noticed there were no stars in the night sky.

CHAPTER THREE

Little Moon at Chilocco

After a year at White Eagle, Elizabeth had changed a great deal. She was no longer her playful self. She had become a very serious little girl. At some point she must have decided that if she was going to be forced into this new world, it would be best for her to follow its rules. She had grown taller, but she was also quieter and more somber as she went about school chores in her little uniform. She rarely laughed and the sparkle in her eyes had dimmed.

One morning, following the five a.m. wake-up bell, change was in the air. A matron was announcing time to get up, wash, and have breakfast. Then, instead of going to the classroom, the children were to return to their dorm room and pack up their belongings—not much, just a few changes of uniforms. They were not allowed any jewelry and certainly no cultural items, ever. At breakfast they whispered among themselves, wondering where they were going. The gossip was wild and scary. At five years old, my grandmother had no idea what any of this meant; she just followed the bigger girls. No letters would be sent to their parents until the children were on their way. The agent wanted to avoid possible uprisings by the angry parents when they learned that their children were being taken away again. They were to enter a new boarding school recently authorized by Congress. For the first time, Little Moon heard the name Chilocco.

When my grandmother was marched outside the White Eagle School that early spring morning, two wagons were waiting for the students. The children had no idea where they were headed; they were simply excited to be outside instead of packed into a single dark schoolroom for most of the day. Soon they were heading north at a slow but steady pace. The first city they passed through was called Cross, later to be named Ponca City after our tribe. As they continued, they entered another small but growing city called Newkirk. Along the route they watched men hard at work building a structure with steel and wooden bars. Later they would learn it was a new railroad. It would run from the north to the south, dividing Indian Territory in half.

In late afternoon, after traveling all day in the uncomfortable wagon, the children finally approached their destination: Chilocco. The year was 1886, and the school had been open to students for two years. A single massive three-story building rose against the sky. To Elizabeth it looked like an island in a sea of prairie. At night Chilocco's lights were the only ones that shone for miles around, so to locals and travelers it became known as the Light on the Prairie.

INTO THE UNKNOWN

Every child's journey to a boarding school was a journey into the unknown. Elizabeth rode by wagon across the prairie. At least the land was familiar to her. For children going to schools farther away, the journey was terrifying. Lakota author Luther Standing Bear wrote about leaving his home in Dakota Territory in 1879. He and other boys from his tribe were fully unprepared for the long trip to Carlisle Indian School in Pennsylvania. At the train station the boys climbed into "a long row of little houses standing on long pieces of iron." When the vehicle pulled away, the children clung to their seats, expecting the worst to happen. After passing the "Smokey City" of Chicago, Luther wrote, "the big boys were singing brave songs, expecting to be killed at any minute." Some feared they would be dumped over the edge of the earth. The journey was the beginning of years of change and anxiety the boys would suffer, separated from their homes, families, and cultures.

A century and a half later, Denise K. Lajimodiere visited her father's boarding school, Chemawa, in Salem, Oregon. She held her breath as a staff member quietly paged through a ledger. "And there he was," wrote Denise, "Leo Joseph Lajimodiere, 1925, Turtle Mountain Agency, Chippewa, nine years old." She spent a heartbreaking day reading records about his years of abuse at the school. Then she walked outside, along the train tracks, for a breath of air. A car pulled up beside her, and a man stepped out. They spoke about Chemawa Indian School. The man said his father had been the conductor for the train that brought the children to the school. "It was so sad; crying, screaming, scared to death, them kids," he told her. He shook his head, got back in his car, and slowly drove away.

Chilocco is actually a Cherokee word that means "big deer." There were truly big plans for the school. It was designed to be one of the largest and most productive government Indian schools authorized by Congress. I call them super schools. In such schools, students would be brought from hundreds of tribes across the United States and housed and educated for an extended time. Chilocco itself was built on 10,000 acres of prime Cherokee land in an area of Indian Territory called the

Panhandle, in present-day Oklahoma. The master plan was to make the school a small self-sufficient city with classrooms, dorms, industrial buildings, and an agricultural center.

At the time Elizabeth was sent to Chilocco, it was simply one huge building containing classrooms, administration offices, and the dormitories, but it would grow. She and her young companions were the first to populate this "super school." They had been abducted from their families on a scale the world had never seen. It was happening across the United States and Canada, with tens of thousands of Indigenous and First Nations children stolen. Already Elizabeth's outward appearance had been changed in such a way that she would never again look like an American Indian child. Instead, she and her companions were but copies of the greater white society.

As they neared the school, the children watched men building a massive structure. The children had no clue what this new construction was, but the commotion and the modern-looking design fascinated them. It would become a small railroad station. Students and supplies shipped across the nation would arrive at the big depot in Arkansas City, eight miles to the north. Then they'd be loaded into another train and sent on a spur, or small rail line, that specifically stopped at Chilocco. Now, the entrance to the school loomed before them. Above rose an entrance gate of black wrought iron. Elizabeth must have been in awe of the metal scrollwork interlaced with flowers. The

43

Entrance to the Chilocco Indian Agricultural School.

name *Chilocco* was neatly centered in the arch high above the road. Elizabeth gazed ahead, the barren drive seeming to travel forever through the tall-grass prairie to the horizon. In the distance she could see just the top of the lone, very tall building. As the wagon rattled along the drive, she began to notice something different. This road was finer than the dirt and loose-gravel roads she had known. It was packed limestone dust, making it as hard and smooth as concrete. The horses' hooves even made a different sound as they clicked on the smooth, solid surface. All the children's eyes were open wide: This was something else! What was this place they had been transported to? Certainly, it was unlike anywhere they had been before.

Soon the children saw wagons filled with young trees to be planted. Unloading the trees were teams of kids who stopped briefly to stare back as the new arrivals passed. The student workers were planting the trees along both sides of the mile-long entrance drive. These trees would grow so tall that they'd bend to touch at the tops, creating a tunnel through which visitors would travel to the big building. Every student would remember the tree tunnel as Chilocco's signature arch. At just five years old, Elizabeth would be in this first class to help plant the famous tree-lined drive. Amid the sadness of separation from her family, watching the tree grow up with her would become a fond memory.

As the wagon continued, Elizabeth was wide-eyed at all the activity around her. On each side of the road several groups of young Indian boys in overalls were building a fence. Each group had a foreman who either worked with the boys or stood by, supervising. All the work was so organized. A little farther on she saw other students building farm ponds. Some students guided big mules that pulled plows. Behind them followed mule-powered bulldozers whose large steel blades in steel frames leveled the plowed earth.

Elizabeth was so excited that she stood up in the wagon and pointed. "Hi^{n}dá!" she cried out in Ponca, forgetting to say "Look!" in English. One of the older Ponca girls quickly reached out and put her hand over Elizabeth's mouth as she pulled Elizabeth into her lap. A matron riding in front turned and scanned the children, scowling. Who had called out in this offensive language? As the older girl cradled her, Elizabeth looked straight ahead with the others, staying silent. She had escaped punishment for now.

Elizabeth saw even more student work groups planting an apple orchard. Beyond that, a large lake, newly dug, was already filled with water. Chilocco was huge, thought my grandmother. Whoever had planned it had thought of everything. There was a wide oval loop that would eventually connect the future campus with the main three-story building. For now, this building would hold both classrooms and dormitories. All around the loop, other buildings were in construction. Every one of the children was in awe of the new school they had been brought to.

While impressive at first sight, Chilocco's layout fit a white man's ideals, not an Indian's. Like Chilocco, other schools such as Carlisle and Phoenix also had square buildings. Square-shaped dorms, dining rooms, and classrooms were filled with neat lines of beds, tables, and desks. The natural land with its rocks and plants was leveled by bulldozers to create neat gardens lined with rows of shrubs and flowers. Things that mattered in the American Indian world were circular in shape: the sky, the sun, the moon, the tepee, the sacred hoop, or medicine wheel, used for health and healing. Majestic buildings and grounds with sharp corners became a prison. Said one Elder, "We are vanishing in this box."

The first building at Chilocco, including the fences that were being built the day Elizabeth arrived.

Before the wagon pulled up to the big building, the children checked on their little medicine bags. An older Ponca girl had carefully hidden Elizabeth's bag inside her packed clothing. Using sign language, she told Elizabeth to be quiet about it. The small bags contained herbs from family members. Each herb would bring protection and comfort. The medicine bag is an example of Pan-Indian culture. Many Indian Nations shared this practice. It had not started with the Ponca, but once adopted, they cherished it as much as did any other tribe. The Ponca bags carried cedar and other herbs. One herb has a scent that Ponca boys especially love as a men's cologne. We call that the grandmother flower. When illness strikes, cedar flower creates an atmosphere where healing can begin. Other personal herbs they carried included some kinds of sage used to cleanse and bless a space. Their little medicine bags were both useful to them and symbols of hope. So the children checked on them and stored them away. Cherished little jewels of their culture hidden in their clothing bundles were all they had to remember of their heritage.

The wagons halted before the building's enormous doors. One by one, the children streamed down and were herded into military lines. Then they marched inside. The entrance hall was huge to the little girls and boys. Matrons and student matrons met them there. The first task was to divide the students into perfect lines of boys on one side and girls on the other. This was no surprise to the students, who had learned military ways at White Eagle. But the next move was shocking.

The lines were ordered to march around the large room and to stop at two large trash bins. As the students passed the bins they were instructed to throw in their personal, hand-packed bundles, including their little hidden medicine bundles. These would later be burned. Some children were almost crying at this point. The matrons knew exactly what they were doing. To them it was just a job well done, their first step in "killing the Indian" in the students. My grandmother recalled the look of satisfaction on their faces.

It might have been worse. In other schools, like Chemawa, children were immediately marched to a bathing area to be scrubbed clean. One boarding school survivor, Elsie, of the Yakima tribe, cried as she told her story. "I was four years old when I was stolen and taken to Chemawa. The matron grabbed me and my sister, stripped off our clothes, laid us in a trough, and scrubbed our genitals with lye soap, yelling at us that we were 'filthy savages, dirty.' I had to walk on my tip toes screaming in pain."

Next, Elizabeth and the students were marched without hesitation to long tables to receive their new Chilocco uniforms. These were laid out by sizes, from the smallest uniforms at one end to the largest at the other. With all the brand-new uniforms and shoes before them, the little girls forgot for a moment their cherished medicine bundles. The boys were just as excited by their new clothes, including new dress boots and work boots. They had never had such a wardrobe. With their new clothes the students were then marched to separate dormitory rooms and assigned their beds. The big girls could no longer give my grandmother a view of the stars at night. She, like everyone else, was assigned one bed in a long row of bunks. Here Elizabeth and the other White Eagle students began to meet many other girls from tribes from all over Oklahoma and the nation.

The excitement of the arrival, the new buildings, the new clothes, and the new students soon began to wear off. All the girls would rise at five a.m., get dressed, make their beds, and carry out chores before classes. These could include brewing coffee for the matrons and helping fix breakfast. Then they'd mop corridors and clean bathrooms. The boys might be assigned to milk the cows at five a.m., then they'd work in the garden or on construction sites. As the days turned to weeks, Elizabeth learned the ins and outs of Chilocco. With their little medicine bundles long gone, the girls tried to find other ways to keep memories alive of their families and homes, but their culture seemed so far away. When they were at White Eagle they were close enough to home to have visits from their parents and other relatives. But now they were miles away. It would take families a day or more to reach the school, then to return home. Parents worked hard to make a living for the rest of the family and they simply could not afford the time or expense to travel to see their children in school. Contact became rare, only through letters or packages.

Separation from beloved parents and grandparents left scars on young children. Julia (not her real name) is a former student of St. Joseph's Catholic Boarding School in Chamberlain, South Dakota, and was happy living with her grandparents. They did not have much, but they had love. One day, a bus came and took her and other little girls away from their families. They drove many miles to the school. There, nuns dragged them off the bus and lined them up. One nun demanded to know who were their parents and grandparents. "Kookum [grandmother] and Mooshum [grandfather]," Julia shyly responded in her native language, Michif, a mixture of Cree, Chippewa, and French. The nun slapped Julia's head with her hand and knocked her to the floor. "You can't talk that language anymore . . ." She demanded the children say the words *grandmother* or *mother* and *grandfather* or *father* in English. All the little girls were frightened. "We didn't know what they were talking about . . . but eventually we learned," Julia said many years later. "A lot of girls cried all the time. I wanted to go home, because I loved my grandparents. We all just thought our [families] deserted us."

Even though their native languages were forbidden, many

children still held them close, speaking only to one another, and in secret. Elizabeth and the other Ponca girls were very careful to hide their language from the matrons. They hid their stories, too.

For every people on Earth, language is our identity and our connection to the world. It helps us communicate, to understand, and to feel close to others. Just imagine you are a little kid of four or five years old. You have grown up learning the language of a loving and close-knit family. Its sounds are beautiful to your ears, and the words have meanings that cannot easily be translated. Such words bring joy and comfort. Then, in a single day, you are taken away from the family you love, and you are told never to speak your language again. Instead, you must speak in the language of the people who kidnapped you.

The new words sound cold and hard. The happy emotion is gone when you speak. And there is an even bigger impact. Your own language carried ancient meanings and connections to Earth and all life. My people are very expressive. We talk with facial and hand gestures. Pointing with our lips is common, while the hands help emphasize what's being said. The children in my grandmother's time were trained to speak English with their hands pressed to their sides. If they used their hands, their hands would be swatted with a ruler. As each generation of Indian children was forbidden to speak the language, it would gradually be lost forever.

THE SWEET SOUND OF LANGUAGE

When children were alone at night, they whispered to each other in their lyrical Ponca language. *Hello. Will you be my friend? What does that mean? Can we go home? Will you tell me a story? Good night.*

Here are a few words and phrases they might have used. The pronunciations, with unique guttural or nasal or whispering sounds, remain a mystery to outsiders. A single word might have two or more meanings depending on the inflection a person uses when saying it. The Ponca treasure their language and do not easily share it. Here is a glimpse.

Aho: a greeting used only by Ponca males

ik^{h}áge: friend

hígo^n: to tell a myth or traditional tale

na'ó^n: to hear; to understand

Dádo^n a: What?

-Á: Oh!

Ă: Yes

Ék^{h}o^{n}he: No indeed!

Hi^{n}dá: Look! Listen!

Hí^{n}dak^{h}é: Let me see! Let us see!

Ágthe shugthé: Come home

Lost with language would also be their stories. Some stories hold the key to passing down our tribal values and ethics. They tell Ponca children who they are, what we expect from life, and how we interact with one another. They tell us the history of our people and what we believe in. They explain small but important things, such as the likes and dislikes that make us Ponca. But the greatest connection to our language and our selfhood is knowledge of our mythology. Those were the stories Elizabeth missed the most.

These stories contain many pearls of wisdom, all told in continuing narratives that are funny, tragic, mystifying, dangerous, and beautiful, oh so beautiful. The stories were told to all children, but it was mainly the role of the girls, then the women, to pass the stories down. Some storytellers were better than others. They could light up a lodge with their explosive facial expressions and hand gestures. Every Ponca mother knew these stories and would tell them to her children in the evening and at bedtime. As she spoke, she would enhance the story with songs, perhaps short little lullabies. Some songs were just rhythms and humming. The storyteller would hum and make a drumming motion on the leg or arm of one of the children listening. The listeners would feel the physical connection to the story and their heritage.

Imagine it is late at night in the Chilocco dorm. The lights are out and the matrons asleep. The little Ponca girls huddle under their covers as an older girl begins to whisper a well-known story in the Ponca language. Such stories soothed my grandmother in those early, lonely days. One, called "Rabbit Catches the Sun," was eventually passed down to me. After college, I collected this and many other stories from my tribe and other tribes around the nation, to preserve and celebrate our cultures. I also became an artist, particularly a sculptor. Today I make sculptures in bronze that celebrate the many myths and histories of the Ponca people. In one of my sculptures, I captured the story of "Coyote and Snake" forever. It is also named "The Orphan and the Wren."

The value of these stories to our culture cannot be measured. The stories are filled with characters who have been with our tribe for generations and generations, perhaps since the start of time. Some of the characters are familiar animals, like Coyote, Rabbit, and Fox. Others are mythic animals that are very hard to describe. All the animals have human traits. That is, they speak Ponca and live in homes much like ours. Some are heroes and some are troublemakers or villains. To get what they want, the tricksters concoct elaborate plans to fool or mislead other characters or humans. Sometimes they don't want anything— just to cause mischief.

Through these stories, Ponca children learn morals and values. They find out what it means to be called a hero or a bad person or a kind person. They learn the importance of treating all people with care and respect. The stories may tell of our

Bronze sculpture of Coyote created by me.

favorite foods found in a certain area during a certain season, or they may tell of disgraceful actions we avoid, such as boasting or lying. The stories may talk about our allies and enemies, or tell of a place where a tribe faced great peril, perhaps war. These stories were so much a part of early life that a child might not have realized how valuable they were to Ponca culture. But Elizabeth and all the students at Chilocco seemed to know that these stories were precious treasures. They had to be protected from the white people. They hid their stories and would only share them in secret spaces far from the matrons' eyes.

Sometimes stories helped children understand what was happening to them and their families. Why were their families forced to move away from their traditional homes? Why were the children taken away to white men's schools? What would happen to all Indian Nations?

For my grandmother, these stories helped her sleep at night and make some sense of the life she was forced to live. Gradually, however, as she lost contact with her family, the soft rhythm of her mother's voice telling stories and singing songs faded away. Many of the stories faded, too. They were replaced by new memories of the white man's European history, of nursery rhymes and fairy tales from Germany and England, and of holidays such as Christmas and Easter, which grew from Christian traditions foreign to her people. Think about this tragedy. We are two different cultures that both revere our stories, our families, our celebrations and traditions, and our sense of self. Why couldn't white society appreciate those Indian traditions instead of destroying them? Why couldn't they incorporate our traditions into white practices to make a richer and more universal society? The loss to Indian Nations has been devastating. But white society will never know the extent of its own loss. White ignorance and dismissal of Indian ways has closed off an extraordinary world of art, culture, ecology, medicine, and spirituality that could have been shared, for everyone's benefit. It will take generations for American Indians to recover. It will take generations more for us to freely share our world again.

There were colder and darker times at Chilocco. Many of the children were homesick. Many tried to run away, only to be tracked down and returned by Indian agents. While some matrons were understanding, others could be cruel. If a homesick child wet their bed at night, the next morning they might be forced to hang up their sheets for all to see. Other children would point and laugh. Food was scarce. One early matron named Emma Sleeth wrote that the food was so "meager, lacking even bread," that the children were always hungry. One boy asked why they would say the blessing, "Sanctify the food for the nourishment of our bodies," when they were not being nourished. Elizabeth and her friends were often hungry, too. Still, Chilocco was considered better than other schools.

Elizabeth Little Cook when she was around fifteen years old.

For Elizabeth, half the day was spent in academic classes and half in vocational classes studying a trade. She learned English and the white man's stories. She learned to follow Chilocco rules, to rise early, to carry out her chores, and to excel in the courses of English, history, and arithmetic. She learned to sew white men's pants and white women's dresses. She learned to bake bread, to brew tea, and to cook recipes without the fresh vegetables, nuts, and meats her family had known. As she lost touch with her own family and Ponca heritage, she became a model student for the matrons. At the age of sixteen, my grandmother herself accepted the position of teacher and matron at Chilocco School. Now she would welcome the new students, and she would teach them how to be a white person.

CHAPTER FOUR

Full Moon

Elizabeth spent twenty-two years at Chilocco, from 1886 to 1908. Eleven of those years were as a student, and eleven were as a matron. During her years at the school, her connections to her family and her heritage faded. In the eyes of the teachers and matrons she was a success story. They had molded Elizabeth into the image of a white person. At last, she came home to rejoin her extended Ponca family, a large set of relatives including aunts, uncles, and cousins. They saw immediately that Elizabeth was in danger of losing who she was forever.

Her sisters, my great-aunts, were especially aware. Creth Little Cook, Annie Little Cook No Ear, and Fannie Little Cook No Ear folded her in their arms and began a quiet and subtle process of trying to bring her back to her heritage. Elizabeth knew she was different. She also must have felt left out of so many things, especially one. As daughters of Chief Sam Little Cook, she and her sisters were allowed to wear special markings. At age twelve, Elizabeth should have received a circular tattoo, centered on her forehead, a symbol of her status as the

Annie Little Cook No Ear, Creth Little Cook, and Fannie Little Cook No Ear (from left to right), with the tattoo on their foreheads symbolizing their status as daughters of a Chief.

daughter of a Chief. Its shape represented the sun. But tattoos were forbidden at boarding school. While Elizabeth was away, her sisters had each received the distinguishing tattoo. They had escaped the white system because when the Indian agent arrived to round up children all those years ago, they were considered too old to be reeducated to white ways. (One sister was already married at the time.) Elizabeth would have worn her tattoo with pride. Unfortunately, upon her return she learned that her time for the ceremony had come and gone, and that it could not be repeated.

Still, her sisters continued gently reminding her of the old ways and of her connection to her family and tribe. They spoke only Ponca, and I remember they wore long Ponca dresses with belled sleeves. Some sleeves had a little ribbon, some had none, and some were laced with elaborate ribbon work and appliqued with beautiful signs and symbols of the clans they were associated with. Each symbol had deep historical and spiritual meanings. The sisters knew that Elizabeth carried her language and traditions inside her.

Yet they also knew that the experience at Chilocco would shape their little sister forever. She had been fully reeducated to live in the white man's culture. Elizabeth continued to speak English. In the nearby city she became an accountant's assistant. Eventually, she became the first Indian woman in Oklahoma to be a notary public, a trusted legal position in the white world.

She intended to raise her children to enjoy such success. It was her sisters who would ensure the Ponca Indian language and culture were not lost to future generations.

THE RETURNED

By the time children finished their boarding school experience, they were young adults. Some took city jobs far from home or enlisted in the military. Those who did go home were met with mixed welcomes from their families. An excited family might come to the train station dressed in traditional blankets, shawls, and moccasins, only to see an unfamiliar young woman step onto the platform in patent leather shoes, silk stockings, a sweeping linen skirt, and a feathered hat. One Indian agent described the scene. "These girls cast their eye upon their parents and stare in horror, then burst into tears. The parents turn away in disgust, returning to their homes, leaving the children to shift for themselves."

No family was at the station to meet Leo Lajimodiere and his sister after their four years at Chemawa Indian School. They had been raised by an old Cree couple after their mother died in the 1918 flu epidemic. Then the couple died while the siblings were at school. They had never known their father, but they went to find him anyway. When they knocked on his door, he simply called to their new stepmother, "Oh! The kids are here." Then Leo, who was thirteen years old, spent the night in a tent in the backyard. He never adjusted to that "home," and he ran away a few months later.

Many students resisted family traditions. They might refuse to take part in tribal dances. They might insist on sleeping in a bed instead of on the floor. They might carelessly toss out precious food because it wasn't the white man's food they were used to. Most students eventually fit in, and they used the boarding school experience to enrich their communities. After leaving Carlisle, Luther Standing Bear became a popular author of articles and books, including *Land of the Spotted Eagle*. He praised his Lakota culture and advocated for Indian rights. Other returnees helped translate complicated white documents. Some became lawyers who stood up for their communities against unfair white laws.

For young Polingaysi Qöyawayma, a Hopi, there was "no turning back" to her people's ways. That phrase later became the title of her book. She had fully accepted Christianity during her years at the Sherman Institute, in California. When she came home, she looked down on traditions. Her parents wanted her to join the sacred Kachina homecoming ceremony, where they would share a meal honoring the Hopi spirits. She told her parents she would not eat food "sacrificed to the devil." Polingaysi soon left her village. She lived with Christian missionaries.

Elizabeth married and bore five children. Two by Narcissis Pensoneau, named Edward and Velma. Velma was my mother and known to her family as Full Moon. Three were by Henry Hernandez, named Daniel, Otilia, and Francis. Elizabeth brought them up on the Ponca Reserve, on the land of her parents, Esther and Sam Little Cook. It was the home she'd been stolen from many years before. While Elizabeth worked in an office in the nearby city, her oldest daughter, Velma, shouldered the household responsibilities.

Born in 1912, Velma Pensoneau would weather rough periods with her family during her early childhood. World War I broke

Elizabeth Little Cook after marriage.

out in 1914 and lasted until 1918, taking the lives of 20 million soldiers and civilians. Near the war's end, an influenza pandemic swept the world, killing 50 million more. After these two devastating events, most Americans embraced a "live for today" attitude, which led the country into the Roaring Twenties. Throughout the 1920s, life in the United States prospered. That is, for white people. In 1920, white women won the right to vote. The economy boomed. New technologies made life easier and more efficient. Better transportation was available, and more people bought cars. Women wore comfortable fashions. Many enjoyed vacations and carefree lifestyles. Not American Indians.

In 1924, we, too, were given the right to vote. Through the

American Indian Citizenship Act, we were made legal US citizens. For us, this did more harm than good. We did not care about electing a white president. We *did* care about keeping our own systems of government and our own laws. Sadly, by being made US citizens with the right to vote, our own Native rights were no longer respected. The US government now controlled us completely. More and more land was stolen from us. We were moved into smaller communities, with fewer opportunities to make a living. The assimilation of our children through boarding schools and the destruction of our culture escalated.

In the 1920s, Ponca families worked hard to make a living on small farms and ranches in Oklahoma. Because the Little Cook farm was on a good-size river, the family was able to grow crops. They hunted. But no one was safe from agents stealing our children and holding back our food rations if they felt we had disobeyed government rules. Other dangers lurked. The state was remote, and it became a perfect hiding place for infamous criminals like Frank Nash and Charles Arthur "Pretty Boy" Floyd. Wanted for bank robbery, illegal alcohol sales, and murder in big cities like Chicago, criminals could easily get lost in our prairie lands. (Velma later learned that she had met Pretty Boy Floyd one day while playing with her friends!) The Osage Nation, which owned lands near the Oklahoma Ponca tribe, was especially at risk. They were wealthy owners of Oklahoma oil fields. Crooked businessmen soon moved in to take those lands for themselves. David Grann's nonfiction book and the 2023 film *Killers of the Flower Moon* tell how white entrepreneurs married into Osage families, then brutally murdered them so they could inherit the oil fields.

In the midst of all this, Velma went to boarding school at Chilocco. She enrolled in 1924, when she was twelve years old. Velma's experience entering Chilocco was not as dramatic as her mother's abduction from her family at the age of four. Things had changed a great deal since then. For one, Velma was older and already attending the local school. After eighth grade, students either went to Ponca City schools or to nearby Chilocco. When it was time to make this choice, Elizabeth steered Velma toward Chilocco. Years later, Elizabeth would also send Otilia, Edward, and Francis to Chilocco. But Velma paved the way. Although it meant separating her daughter from her culture, Elizabeth considered her own twenty-two years at Chilocco as happy and productive. She felt it would be an advantage for Velma to learn to live in the white world, too. Soon, a Chilocco representative came to interview Velma as a potential student. It was like being recruited, Velma recalled. She was accepted, and she spent the coming weeks listening to Elizabeth's stories and advice about the school.

The day finally came. Velma's ride to Chilocco was far different from Elizabeth's fearful trip in the back of a horse-drawn wagon so many years before. Now, her stepfather, Henry, drove

Velma and her mother there in a Ford Model T. As they passed the miles of trees and plains, Elizabeth's thoughts wandered to days long ago. Velma looked out the window, with feelings that wavered between fear and hope. Whatever Chilocco had in store for her, Velma was resolved to work hard and to make the best of it. As the oldest daughter, she was used to working in challenging conditions at home. Although her parents were good to her, her stepfather could be harsh. He had a high work standard and held her responsible for most of the housework. Still, given the hard times other Indian families faced, Velma knew they were simply lucky to have the life they had.

When they pulled through the Chilocco gates and started down the mile-long drive, Velma gazed around in awe. Forming an arch above them were the trees her mother had helped plant in her early days at Chilocco. No matter what Velma had heard of Chilocco, she was not ready for the booming world she saw before her. In the two decades since Elizabeth had left Chilocco, the school had become huge and prosperous. It was now a self-contained farming community covering 10,000 acres. The administration had used the students as free laborers to plant crops, care for livestock, and build barns, stables, silos, and outbuildings. Food the students produced was sold at local markets to keep Chilocco running.

But reminders of the oppression of Velma's people were everywhere. As they traveled down the tree-lined drive, a herd of Morgan horses ran alongside the car, on the other side of a strong fence. The Morgan breed, developed in Vermont, was used in warfare by the US Cavalry to keep up with the American Indians' faster breeds. Around the grounds, several large wells were fed naturally by artesian springs. Young Indian laborers had dug the wells by hand. The largest was thirty feet in diameter and at least thirty feet deep. Students had then lined them with rock so they constantly stayed full of water. Students had also built a large water tower and pumped water from the well to fill it. Laborers had planted an orchard with rows of pear, peach, and apple trees, then fully irrigated the land. A huge lake dug by students covered the east side of the campus.

Student laborers had also built the campus buildings and now maintained them. Dorms, classrooms, a cafeteria, and an administration building encircled a central, oval-shaped park. A

The Chilocco Indian Agricultural School campus.

huge power plant supplied electricity and heat to all the buildings. Beyond the main campus, Chilocco boasted some of the most beautiful farm buildings in the country, one for every agricultural purpose. Barns for dairy cattle, hogs, mules, and heavy equipment. Stables and a farrier shop for horses. Huge chicken houses with dozens of species of chickens. Students learned leather-making and created everything from saddles to harnesses for horses and mules. In 1924, Chilocco was celebrated as the only agricultural school like it in the world.

The design was ingenious and intended to make the community fully self-sufficient. When my mother arrived and checked in, she felt like she was dreaming. In later years, she said she thought she had died and they sent her to a luxurious resort. With all the hardships she had endured growing up, this was completely new to her. She was shown to her dormitory, where she had her own bed. The floors were tiled. There was indoor plumbing. It was warm in her room. No more carrying endless armfuls of heavy wood. No more toting water. She would be given chores, but other children would be helping with the same chores. Her roommates were children her own age, who would become lifelong friends. She immediately loved it, and she prospered. Yes, there were endless bells and constant marching around campus and from class to class, but to her that was easy.

In such a comfortable atmosphere it was easy to give over to the white man's ways. It was not until later that she realized the changes happening to her would affect her for the rest of her life. As in all boarding schools, she was called only by her American name, Velma. No longer was she called Full Moon. But her Ponca name remained quietly inside her. So did her language and sense of spirituality.

Although a government school, Chilocco was administered by the Quakers, who were a stern people. As in other religious-run schools, the instructors followed the regulations set by the government. Children were forbidden to speak their Native language or practice Native singing or dancing. Any form of American Indian spiritualism was not allowed in any government boarding school, certainly not at Chilocco. Instead, students were sent to Sunday school and church services. Some were nondenominational (meaning for all Christians), while others were for Catholics only.

Christianity was not new to Velma. Her mother, Elizabeth, had adopted the Catholic faith when she married her second husband, Henry Hernandez. She wanted Velma to follow it, too. At Chilocco, Velma attended Catholic Mass. She memorized their prayers and songs. She listened to the sermons about following in the footsteps of Christ and living a good life. Still, Velma often felt empty hearing their words. Many other children clung to the comfortable Christian faiths they learned at Chilocco as their own Native faiths slipped away. But Velma never did.

The Ponca faith is both simple and complex compared to Christian faiths. At its center is the universal concept of

Wa KoN Da, or the Great Spirit. All the Ponca churches use Wa KoN Da as the name of their god. Through time, religious people would say that Wa KoN Da is the day that follows the night. It is that which causes movement in all things. Wa KoN Da is neither a man nor a woman. It has no physical being. We consider it the Creator Spirit that made the universe and all that is in it. Wa KoN Da also created the Spirit World, which may contain endless worlds.

The old Ponca spirituality has no written bible. All moral and ethical teachings have been by word of mouth. Like most good teachings, the code of ethics asks the Ponca people to follow these rules for useful living. Jews and Christians might recognize a similar code in their Ten Commandments.

1. Have one God, Wa KoN Da.

2. Do not kill.

3. Do not steal.

4. Be good to one another.

5. Do not talk about one another.

6. Do not be greedy.

7. Respect the sacred Pipe.

8. Do not be lazy.

9. Talk to your children.

10. Be prepared, educate yourself.

11. Keep your Ponca language.

The old beliefs were practiced both alone and in social gatherings. The most spiritual Elders would say, "We pray with every step we take and every movement we make." Even today, every Ponca event begins with prayer. Business meetings, dances, games, sporting events, and certainly powwows and cultural events include prayer. Some believe we are close to God because of what we do for others. It is a belief passed down through generations. Others are born into a spiritual clan. Their lineage gives them the right to carry forth the spirituality of our culture. We all accept this. A holy person from the clan may burn a certain herb and fan the smoke onto the clan as a blessing. New Year's Eve is a time when many people gather to receive such a blessing. When Velma left home, she carried spiritual items from her clan that helped her connect with Wa KoN Da and to keep her from harm.

The teachers at Chilocco came from various Christian backgrounds and taught about their faiths in Sunday school. Besides Quakers, there were Catholics, Baptists, Methodists, and members of the Church of the Nazarene. Velma watched the different ways they worshipped and heard the prayers they said. She learned about their Bible. At mealtimes she joined in the grace, "For all Thy bounty's store, Lord, we thank Thee ever more." But all the while she held on to her own beliefs. Just as her aunts had taught her, the Ponca Code of Ethics was her faith. Quietly, she practiced its teachings.

Despite the spiritual teachings different from her own, Velma loved her experience at Chilocco. Her older brother, Edward, was a student there, too, and they spent time together. Compared with the demands her stepfather made at home, Velma found the chores at Chilocco easy. Later in life she and her Chilocco roommate, Amy Homaratha, of the Otoe-Missouria Tribe, would sit in our yard on a summer night, laughing and talking until dawn about their school days. You could never say a bad word about Chilocco around Velma. It helped that her mother, Elizabeth, had been a matron. Matrons always watched out for one another's children. Velma was liked and protected by the staff. They also respected the relationships she developed with other students.

Mom was known as a "tough girl" who would fight a boy quicker than another girl. But she was not a bully. She protected weaker students, and they knew they could go to her with their problems. Velma was aware that other children had come from less fortunate families. Some arrived at the school starving. Others brought illness, such as influenza, diphtheria, or consumption (tuberculosis). These diseases would spread through the dormitories, killing students. Even then, my mother wasn't afraid to help nurse them. This was a trait she carried through her life as a social worker for the state of Oklahoma on Indian issues. Later, she became the first Ponca entrepreneur to own her own restaurant, and she continued helping others.

EPIDEMIC

Epidemics swept through many schools. Poor nutrition and long work hours wore down students' immune systems. Dormitories were not well ventilated, and beds were lined so closely together that children coughed and sneezed on one another, spreading infection. Diseases included pneumonia, measles, mumps, and meningitis. Children contracted trachoma, which causes blindness, and jaundice, a liver disease that causes the skin to turn yellow. Consumption was the most contagious—and the most life-threatening. The disease attacked a child's lungs. Gradually, the child wasted away, coughing up blood. Death was inevitable. Many children who had consumption asked to return home to die. Another form of consumption, called scrofula, attacked the lymph nodes and caused sores on the face and neck. One child at Carlisle, Minnie Tsaitkopeta, begged her family to allow her to come home when she had the disease. "You know how Clara's neck was?" she wrote. "Well, my neck is not well. The thing inside that makes sores is getting big, and they will never take good care of me. I shall fail in health. I am already failing. This is not a place for weak people."

To the horror of Denise K. Lajimodiere, a smallpox epidemic broke out at Chemawa Indian School while her father and his sister were there, in 1927. They survived, but they never mentioned it to her. When she later visited the school to find out more about their story, she discovered a newspaper clipping telling of the outbreak. So many children died that the school was shut down for a while. After that, two more wings were added to the Chemawa hospital so patients could spread out and be less contagious. Any outbreak at a boarding school ended in mass death. Some schools tried to send sick children home before they died, to keep their death rate low for official records. If they returned home, students might spread the illness through their families and communities. The sick children who stayed at the schools were later buried there, often in unmarked graves.

Epidemics were one of the many horrors children faced during the boarding school era. Since the founding of Carlisle in 1879, greater America knew nothing about the poor conditions and physical and mental abuse that ran rampant in many boarding schools. Now, in the 1920s, information was leaking out to the public. A white policymaker named John Collier was the executive secretary for a government organization called the American Indian Defense Association. He was angered by the general prosperity of whites in the 1920s compared with the extreme poverty of American Indians. He grew more angered by boarding school reports. At last, he started his own publicity campaign to raise America's awareness. Collier's team, called the Committee of One Hundred, issued a report. That report was the catalyst for a more in-depth government report, which would shake the boarding school system to its core: the Meriam Report.

Commissioned in 1926 by the Department of the Interior Secretary Hubert Work, the Meriam Report was officially called *The Problem of Indian Administration*. A team of scholars from a government research institute, today's Brookings Institution, were led by legal expert Lewis Meriam. They traveled to twenty-six states, assessing the condition of American Indian life. The results were appalling. In a forty-one-part report, America learned of the treatment forced upon the First Peoples of this nation. Broken treaties. Deceptive policies. Unfair legal actions. Decimation. Death. As the rest of the nation flourished, the conditions of Indian lands and communities, health care, economy, families, and education were found deplorable. Especially the state of boarding schools.

The report revealed the "care of Indian children in boarding schools" as "grossly inadequate." Not only were teachers and curriculum substandard, but living conditions ranged from vermin-infested food to filthy latrines to nonexistent medical care. Horrifying excerpts about student treatment included: "Punishments of the most harmful sort are bestowed in sheer ignorance; we should hardly have children from the smallest to the largest of both sexes lined up in military formation . . . In nearly every boarding school one will find children of 10, 11, and 12 spending four hours a day in . . . heavy industrial work—dairy, kitchen work, laundry, shop. The work is bad for children of this age, especially children not physically well nourished; most of it in no sense is educational . . . [It is] a violation of child labor laws . . ."

The report recommended keeping young children at home, in local schools, and sending only older children to boarding schools; doing away with studies that stressed only white cultural values; and, finally, helping Indian families keep their culture while understanding white ways. The report was far from righting centuries of wrongs that started in the 1400s. But it was a beginning. By 1929, reforms were making headway under Indian Commissioner Charles Rhoads. Boarding schools were getting better food and medical care. Curriculums were revised. Some of the worst-reported schools were closed.

After the initial hype died down, however, many of the remaining schools slipped back into their old ways. Still, America's eyes had been opened and there was no turning back. Franklin Delano Roosevelt was elected US president in 1932. He had a plan, called the New Deal, that would look out for the country's best interests. That included American Indians. In 1933, Roosevelt named John Collier, who had first campaigned for Indian rights in 1926, as the new Indian commissioner. Collier was ready. An energetic and impassioned advocate for American Indian rights, his changes would shake up complacent school administrators and jump-start boarding school reform.

John Collier following his appointment as commissioner of Indian Affairs.

During my mother's years at Chilocco, she knew little about the Meriam Report. She did not notice that the boarding school era would soon begin its decline. She was a hard worker. She followed the rules. She was a social person involved in her immediate world. Just as the government had originally hoped, she embraced her experience. She assimilated into white society, for the time being. In the end, however, her cultural inheritance would prove stronger.

Later, when Velma came home after graduation, her aunts treated her much as they had her mother, Elizabeth. Once again Velma was known as Full Moon. The aunts helped her renew her connection to the old Ponca ways. They reminded my mother that practicing kindness and respect are key to living our spiritual life. Just as important to spirituality is speaking our language and using our words to share our beliefs with our children. Despite English training in school, my mother never lost her own language. She would say she was not fluent, which I never understood. I listened to her speak Ponca to me and to her friends and relatives for hours at a time. Once in a while, she would use an English word or two. But because of her aunts, she retained her spiritual connection to her Ponca language and philosophy.

After my great-aunts passed away, Velma's husband (and my father), Lee Otis Jones, would help her keep her spiritual outlook and practice. By the time Velma entered the fourth season of her life, meaning her final years, she had long known that Christianity

Velma Pensoneau.

Lee Otis Jones.

with its rote prayers and ceremonies could never satisfy her. She needed a deeper connection to everything around her, to the world that was seen and unseen. That is our Ponca faith. It is very personal. It is Nature itself. Velma would still go to church services with her friends who followed Christian faiths. Many of those women were Elders and the judges of the tribe. Their bonds of friendship were strong. But in her private life my mother fully embraced her Native spirituality. Later, she shared this gift with me. She brought me up in the Ponca faith, and I have received its benefits. Like my mother, Full Moon, many other boarding school students quietly held on to their beliefs. Change was coming, but decades of rough road lay ahead.

CHAPTER FIVE

Athletes & Soldiers: The Warrior Spirit

Chilocco was organized like a military base. Everything ran by
the bell. When to get up, when to eat, when to go to class. Each
class began and ended with a bell. This was the everyday routine, except for one day a year, in the springtime.

On that day, in every building, the children were awakened
by the matrons hurrying through the halls, calling out, "IT'S
PLAY DAY!" The children would pile out of their bunks in
excitement! No bells, no lines, no drills. Nothing was like any
other day of the year. On this day the girls could wear pants!
Breakfast was prepared and packed into paper bags so the students could eat on the run. The whole school was different that
day. Mixing of students was usually forbidden, but on that day
the boys and girls could hang out together, all day long if they
wanted to. They could go fishing in the big lake, or boating, or
take part in a whole list of student activities. There would be
cookouts with hot dogs and chips. There was even soda pop.
Normally, those things were strictly prohibited.

Play Day was an institutional tradition at Chilocco as far back as anyone could remember. The date was kept highly secret. Only the staff were involved in planning the whole event. In my mother's time, the workers created a play area right on Chilocco Creek, a mile from the campus. There they built a bonfire and set up tables where meals could be served. The workers made long swings with ropes tied to large tree limbs that hung over the water. Students could swing out over the creek and drop in. Swimming and games were full-day events. There were tug-of-war matches between various groups of boys and girls, and the losers were pulled into the creek. There were gunnysack races and athletic games of all sorts. It was a day like no other at Chilocco, and the kids and adults all loved it.

Another more traditional Chilocco sport was the winter rabbit hunt. Each boy would find a "rabbit club." This was no more than a two-foot-long, curved stick with a stone or other little weight tied to the end. Then up to a hundred boys would form a long line across the prairie. The boys would space themselves so that they could fling the stick at the rabbit as it ran between them. Most rabbits would run like lightning away from the lines, but the boys closest to a rabbit would still throw their sticks, hoping to hit it. Many times they did. The sticks worked like boomerangs. On a successful hunt the boys could bring back dozens of rabbits to the cooks, who made large vats of rabbit stew.

Play for pure fun was rare at Chilocco or at any boarding school. But playing sports for competition took on an important role. Several boarding schools, including Carlisle, Haskell, and Chilocco, had long been famous for their men's teams. Through the 1930s, women's teams would also gain prominence. Boarding school reforms, which had started with the Meriam Report, would grow. In 1933, John Collier struck down laws prohibiting American Indians from practicing their religion and culture. He hired American Indians to work in the Bureau of Indian Affairs. He pushed Congress to pass the Indian Reorganization Act of 1934, protecting tribal lands and governments, and boosting economic development. Most important, Collier took a magnifying glass to boarding schools. He supported the Meriam Report recommendations: Only older children should attend the schools. Students should learn and practice their heritage. Physical and mental health were priorities, meaning good food, good care, and no abuse, period. Those schools that didn't pass muster were closed. By 1935, boarding school enrollment was cut nearly by half. The schools that remained had a chance to shape up and offer positive education for the future. Many students found opportunities to grow. Those who benefited from this new era included my mother, Velma.

My mother participated in as many sports as were available to the young girls at Chilocco at that time. In the 1920s into the 1930s, sports for girls anywhere were limited. But Chilocco had a gym where girls competed among themselves in games such as basketball. Outdoors they played softball, dodgeball, and kickball. They didn't have organized teams with coaches. They didn't play scheduled games against other schools and towns like the boys did. But that would change.

The boys' teams included basketball, baseball, and football. But it was boxing that stood out at Chilocco. The school's team was highly successful and widely known to have the best boxers in America. In 1936, Chilocco boxers won the first Oklahoma Golden Gloves team championship, and they went on to win national Golden Gloves competitions. Among the students taking home the top prizes were young boxers from tribes including the Comanche, Chickasaw, Ponca, Cheyenne, Otoe-Missouria, and many others.

One story Velma cherished while at Chilocco was the day that the sports champion Jim Thorpe and his wife, Iva Miller, came to visit their daughter, Grace. Jim was a graduate of Carlisle Industrial School, in Pennsylvania, but he had grown up in Oklahoma and later his family moved there. He and his wife decided to send Grace to Chilocco. (Iva herself had attended Chilocco before transferring to Carlisle, where she met Jim.) A member of the Sac and Fox Nation of Oklahoma, Jim was an All-America football player and Olympic champion. The entire school turned out that day to greet him. At 6'1", he towered over the students. My mother recalled having the opportunity to meet Jim and shake his huge hand. Despite being a strong young woman, she said her hand felt small and fragile inside his.

Jim Thorpe with Grace.

BRIGHT PATH

Jim Thorpe began his rise to athletic fame in 1907, a few years after he entered Carlisle Industrial School in Pennsylvania. The story goes that one day he was walking past the track in his school uniform and decided to join the high-jump practice. When he made a jump 5'9" high, the team was amazed. The coach, Glenn Scobey "Pop" Warner, signed Jim up. Soon, Jim was breaking records in track and field events, winning medal after medal. He ran the 100-yard dash in 10 seconds flat. He ran a mile in 4 minutes and 35 seconds. He pole-vaulted 11 feet into the air and threw a javelin 163 feet straight forward.

Mostly, Jim wanted to play football. Pop Warner kept saying no. What if Jim were tackled and injured and could no longer compete in track and field? "Nobody is going to tackle Jim," the young athlete assured Pop. Jim soon proved that no other players could get close as he ran the field. When Carlisle played the Army team from West Point, Jim went head to head against the future general and US president Dwight D. Eisenhower. The president later recalled that Jim "could do anything better than any other football player I ever saw." Jim went on to college at Haskell Indian Nations University in Kansas. He was named an All-America college athlete. Although football remained Jim's favorite sport, he also excelled in lacrosse and ballroom dancing, and he played professional baseball. In the 1912 Olympic Games he won two gold medals in track and field. At one point he competed in mismatched shoes because his own had been stolen. Nothing could stop Jim. A fellow Olympic gold medalist called him "the greatest athlete who ever lived." It is fitting that the name given to him at birth was Wa-Tho-Huk. It means "path lit by a great flash of lightning," or "Bright Path."

Jim Thorpe's sports story began in the early 1900s, when he first attended Haskell Institute in Lawrence, Kansas. Like Chilocco and other government boarding schools, Haskell's classes and its entire system of living were based on a military system. Students wore uniforms. Their hair was cut short. Bells announced every class and every hour of the day. Students

Jim Thorpe.

marched everywhere. Marching wasn't just standing up straight and picking up your knees as you moved along by yourself. Students had to form straight lines and keep in step with every other person around them, no matter where they were going. Discipline ruled the day. Jim Thorpe's early military training at Haskell would serve him later. In his early teens, Jim dropped out of Haskell and worked on a ranch for a while. Then, in 1904, at the age of sixteen, he made his way to Carlisle.

As the first off-reservation federal boarding school, Carlisle had a rigid, regimented format, the model upon which Haskell and all other schools were based. Carlisle also had the greatest reputation for its competitive sports program. The military mindset used in the boarding schools was good training for a strong athlete. Like a soldier, an athlete was required to be prompt and disciplined, and to be part of a team. At Carlisle, Jim excelled in track and field, football, baseball, lacrosse, and even ballroom dancing, which was considered a sport in those days.

Although Jim was not a student at Chilocco, his sports legacy had a lasting influence on the young athletes at the school. When Grace Thorpe attended Chilocco, she represented what all the students, especially the girls, could accomplish. Grace pursued sports at Chilocco, but she went on to make her mark in other ways. She became an army officer, a lawyer, and a tribal judge for her Sac and Fox people, renowned for protecting their heritage and the environment of her homeland.

WORLD CHAMPIONS

Visitors to the 1904 St. Louis World's Fair were fascinated by a new game called basketball that was still being introduced to the world. Spectators were even more fascinated by the athletes playing the game. Not only were they women, they were Native Americans. They had trained at an isolated boarding school in Montana named Fort Shaw. The team's ten players had come from seven different Indian nations. Some tribes had been longtime adversaries. Now they came together to play a spellbinding game that made sports pages across the nation. The girls were so swift and skilled as they outplayed one white team that the *Bozeman Chronicle* reported, "The white girls were never in the game at all." Not only did the players excel in basketball, they amazed their audiences with accompanying performances, including mandolin concerts, gymnastic routines, and daring pantomimes. Emblazoned on trophies were the girls' names: Minnie Burton (Lemhi Shoshone); Genie Butch, Sarah Mitchell, Katie Snell, and Nettie Wirth (Assiniboine); Genevieve Healy (Gros Ventre); Belle Johnson (Piegan); Rose LaRose (Shoshone-Bannock); and Flora Lucero and Emma Sansaver (Chippewa-Cree). In their book, *Full Court Quest,* authors Linda Peavy and Ursula Smith tell the team's extraordinary story. After storming across Montana, they became the state's first basketball champions. Then they took on teams in North Dakota and Minnesota. At the 1904 World's Fair they emerged women champions of the world.

Fort Shaw girls' basketball team.

My mother was a pioneer in building the sports program in the 1930s at Chilocco. But it was long after my mother's time that women were recognized for their part in contributing to Chilocco's legacy in sports. The program would go on to include softball, baseball, football, boxing, track and field, swimming, water sports, and ballroom dancing. Eventually, the sports teams competed widely, with other teams across the state. Later, traditional dancing was accepted, too. Students had the opportunity to compete in the Fancy Dance, Single Bustle, Straight Dance, and others. They performed meaningful steps and motions that were part of their heritage.

Some students, like Jim Thorpe, were successful at channeling the school's military training into athletics. Frank Jude, a Minnesota Ojibwe, played baseball at Carlisle before he joined the Cincinnati Reds in 1906 and became an outfielder. Charles Albert Bender was also a Minnesota Ojibwe who attended Carlisle in the early 1900s. He entered the Baseball Hall of Fame after his star career as a pitcher with the Philadelphia Athletics. Throughout his life, his white colleagues called him "Chief." This derogatory nickname was used despite his enormous success as a pitcher, a coach, and a recruiter. Decades later, Billy Mills was on the scene as an Olympic gold medalist in track and field. An Oglala Sioux from the Pine Ridge Reservation in South Dakota, Billy attended Haskell in the 1950s. Three times he was named All-America athlete. After graduating he served in the marines. Then, in 1964, he became the first American and first Native American to win a gold medal at the Olympic Games in the 10,000-meter race. His record holds today.

In all the schools, athletic discipline was closely linked to military indoctrination. Students had different memories of their experiences. Some say they liked following rules. They found the discipline useful in their future education and jobs. Some used it to manage their families. When my mother shared her stories with me about the military life at Chilocco, she chose to share positive times. One of our tribal Elders, Metha Gives Water Collins, also thrived in this environment. She remembered the military training when she was at Chilocco in 1914. "We had officers—captains; first and second lieutenants; first, second, third sergeants. We marched to school, work, and to Leupp Hall. In this military rule of school I became first sergeant." During World War I, Metha became "boss" of the sewing room, where the girls sewed and knitted for the US troops.

Other students had less fond memories. One student in the 1920s and 1930s named Curtis Carr told stories to his daughter K. Tsianina Lomawaima many years later. She recorded his stories and the stories of sixty other children in her book about Chilocco, *They Called It Prairie Light*. The children remembered that the bugle sounded twenty-two times a day. There were calls for wakeup (reveille), for assembly, for all the meals (mess calls), for classes, and finally for bedtime. Discipline started with getting out of bed. One student from the Cherokee Nation recalled that you had to strip your bed, then flip over your mattress. When you made up the bed, the sheet and blanket had to stretch super tight across the mattress. So tight that you could throw a quarter on it, and it would bounce. Then the matrons and other officers came to check. If they threw down a quarter and it didn't bounce, they'd tear up the bed and make you fix it again.

Then there was a white-glove test. The dormitory matrons would run their gloved fingers over door frames and under beds checking for dust. All the time, students stood at attention, sweating in their uniforms and hoping they wouldn't get a demerit. If they did, they would have to be punished with duties such as polishing the hallways on their hands and knees.

Every morning the students had to dress in military uniforms and go outside and march in formations called close-order drill. Rain or shine, hot or cold. They marched shoulder to shoulder and carried guns. Then they stood at attention and performed drills to show how they could handle the weapons. On Sundays, the boys and girls would compete in dress parades. One former student from the Creek Nation was just nine years old but felt like he was already in the army. He and all the other kids had to wear old World War I uniforms with wrapped leggings and high-button collars. Even the littlest among them carried heavy army rifles as they stood at attention and marched around the drilling field.

Leo Lajimodiere was nine years old when he arrived at Chemawa Indian School. He remembered marching everywhere he went. "We had to look straight ahead," he told his daughter Denise. "Couldn't even move our eyes or we'd get hit." He marched with a small wooden rifle when he first got there at age nine. As he grew older, he was issued a regular rifle. The guns were never loaded, and the kids never were trained to shoot. Many of them had already learned to hunt at home and would use those skills later.

Marching became so ingrained in the students that some couldn't break the habit even when they went out in public.

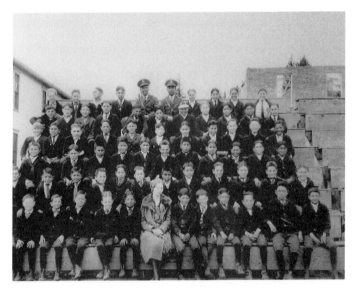

Leo Lajimodiere at Chemawa. He's in the second row up
from the bottom, fourth boy from the right.

For Anna Moore Shaw, who went to Phoenix Indian School in Arizona, marching was hard at first. But once she and her friends learned it, it became automatic. All the students were allowed to visit the nearby town once a month. On one visit, a loudspeaker from a store was attracting customers with loud band music. Anna was horrified when she and her friends started marching. "Try as hard as we could, we just couldn't get out of step. It was Impossible! We'd try to take long strides to break the rhythm, but soon we would fall back into step again. How embarrassing it was!"

While military training was a large part of all schools, Chilocco was the only American Indian boarding school with an active unit of the US Army National Guard. One unit was officially established on the Chilocco campus during World War II. Almost 100 percent of the student body joined it. Some fought in Europe or the Pacific. Others worked for the troops on the home front, in factories or road construction. In the 1950s, during the Korean War, Chilocco's unit became known as Company C in the 279th Infantry Regiment. At school, the budding soldiers proudly called it "Charlie" Company. At any moment Chilocco students were ready to join. The school already ran as a military base; officially enlisting in the armed services was just the next step.

During Velma's time at the school, Chilocco had military ranking from private to captain. Velma made it to captain, the highest ranking for a student. By the time my older brother and sister went to Chilocco in the 1950s, the ranks were discontinued.

Still, they marched everywhere they went. In my mother's time, right before World War II, one of my uncles, along with other students from Chilocco, went directly into the military after graduation, enlisting in the Oklahoma National Guard. Years later, my cousin recalled my uncle's story that in boot camp they could hear the white kids crying because they were homesick. Not the Indian kids. They were already accustomed to being in a military environment far away from family and friends. They were the perfect preconditioned soldiers. Leo Lajimodiere always said the army was a piece of cake compared to boarding school.

John Collier's Indian Reorganization Act (IRA) and related work may have helped diminish the role of boarding schools in the 1930s and 1940s. It may have helped open up new opportunities. But many of the schools continued on the path they'd taken since the 1800s. Young students still had to learn English. They had to practice someone else's religion. They still had to labor in fields and on construction sites. They had to learn military ways. They had to be white.

First, the government had taken children from their homes and families. Then they had stripped them of their Native identity. Now they trained them as soldiers who would fight for a country that so deeply disrespected them. It might be surprising that those young students still wanted to serve. But they did. They willingly went to military offices to enlist and to fight in World Wars I and II and later wars. Part of the reason may be that the military life was the only life they knew. But there is another, more important reason.

Through time, every tribe has held the sacred understanding that they must protect their families and homeland. This dedication was passed on to every generation, even when their homeland was taken over by the US government. By fighting, the warriors were protecting their own people. They were bringing honor to their community. They were filling their families with pride. If you look at wars from World War I through today, you will see that American Indian communities send more soldiers to fight than any other community does. When the soldiers return, they are more honored by their people than military veterans in any other community in the nation. A warrior, regardless of gender, is a hero.

Ernest Childers, Jack C. Montgomery, and Charles George are three of Chilocco's heroes. Starting as students at the school, Ernest and Jack went on to serve in the Oklahoma National Guard, then on the front lines in World War II. Charles did not attend Chilocco but was assigned to Company C after he enlisted and served in Korea in 1952. They all received the Congressional Medal of Honor, the highest honor America awards to its greatest war heroes. The stories of Second Lieutenant Childers, First Lieutenant Montgomery, and Private First Class George are among the most harrowing.

Ernest Childers, a member of the Muskogee tribe, had recently come to Chilocco when he enlisted in the National Guard in 1937. Unrest was brewing in Europe, and there was talk of war. It wasn't long before World War II broke out. Soon, Ernest and his unit were on the way to fight Nazi forces in Fascist Italy. Ernest was ready. He had always been a good shot. As a young boy he had used a gun to hunt rabbits for family meals. But his family could afford just one bullet a day. Ernest soon learned to aim and fire with almost 100 percent accuracy so his family could eat. His training was never more vital than on September 22, 1943, when a nest of German machine gunners was raining down fire on American troops.

Ernest had just broken his foot and was hobbling, but that didn't stop him. He led eight other men up a hill and across a cornfield, firing as they went. Bullets from two enemy snipers whizzed past Ernest, just missing him. Ernest aimed and shot

Ernest Childers receiving the Medal of Honor in April 1944.

them both. Farther up the hill his group made a surprise attack on the machine gun nest. The gunners turned to fire, but Ernest was faster. He took out all but one. The other was shot by one of his team. He didn't stop. Near the hilltop an enemy soldier was trying to report the action to headquarters. Ernest captured him. Through his brave actions, Ernest was able to save scores of US troops from harm. On the battlefield, Ernest was awarded the Congressional Medal of Honor. He was the first American Indian in World War II to receive the medal, "for exceptional leadership, initiative, calmness under fire, and conspicuous gallantry [that] were an inspiration to his men."

Not far from Ernest's company in Fascist Italy, Jack Montgomery soon made history, too. Jack had also enlisted in the National Guard. He was quickly promoted to lieutenant and led a rifle platoon across the Italian countryside in early 1944. Just before dawn one morning, Jack could see in the distance a group of Nazi soldiers blocking Company C's path. Seizing a rifle and several hand grenades, he crawled alone through a ditch until he was in range. Then he threw his grenades and began firing. In a few minutes he had killed or captured the entire group. But he wasn't finished. After he delivered the captured Nazis, Jack went back to the scene of the attack. He had noticed a house that looked suspicious, likely a good hiding place for other Nazi snipers. Again he ordered his men to cover him with machine gun fire as he crawled through the shallow ditch

Jack C. Montgomery in 1944.

toward the enemy. He charged the house alone, attacking with all his might. Soon the Nazi soldiers emerged, their hands in the air. For his "fearless, aggressive, and intrepid actions," he received the Medal of Honor from President Franklin Roosevelt later that year.

Charles George grew up in North Carolina, a member of the Cherokee tribe. Too young for World War II, he enlisted in time for the Korean War in 1952, when he was twenty years old. Although he had attended the Cherokee School at Qualla Boundary, North Carolina, he was assigned to Chilocco's Charlie Company as a private first class. Charles's birth name was Tsali, the name of a legendary Cherokee hero of the early 1800s. That hero had saved many

Cherokee people from being removed to Oklahoma on the Trail of Tears from 1837 to 1839. In the end, Tsali sacrificed his life. Now, true to his birth name, the twentieth-century Tsali, or Charles, became a force in Charlie Company. He was committed to keeping his people safe at home and carrying on his Cherokee warrior tradition.

On November 30, 1952, Charles joined a raid to capture a Korean enemy soldier so the officers could interrogate him. His party climbed a rugged slope, dodging heavy mortar and machine gun fire. At the top, they leapt into the trenches and fought in hand-to-hand combat with the enemies inside. After capturing the prisoner, the company began to withdraw. Charles and two

Charles George.

others stayed behind, watchful. They wanted to ensure their comrades' safe retreat. Suddenly, a grenade from enemy lines landed at their feet. Pushing the others out of the way, Charles threw himself down, fully covering it. He took the full blast and died shortly after. For Charles's "indomitable courage, consummate devotion to duty, and willing self-sacrifice," his family later accepted the Congressional Medal of Honor in his name. His ancestor, Tsali, would have been proud.

Scores of former students from Chilocco have received medals or citations for their wartime service, from World War I, 1914–1918, through the Vietnam War, 1955–1975. Many have given the ultimate gift to the nation: their lives. Their skill as soldiers comes from their training as athletes and soldiers at Chilocco. But their dedication and fearlessness in battle comes from our long warrior culture, ingrained from childhood. The story is the same across the nation. Try as they might to "kill the Indian" in us, no schools could ever take away our warrior spirit.

While so many American Indians were fighting in the World War II and Korean theaters, those on the home front were experiencing a different kind of battle. Since its passing, the Indian Reorganization Act had championed tribal autonomy and the return of tribal lands. Its funding had helped boost economies on Indian reservations. Its policy in boarding schools and mainstream society had encouraged renewed respect for ancient cultures and practices. But not all Indians agreed with the policy. Many were now so fully assimilated that they wanted to live in white society. They resented being grouped into needy clans that could not survive without government help.

CODE TALKERS: THEIR LANGUAGE WON WARS

While many American Indian warriors were winning medals on the front lines for their skill and bravery, many others were using their language to fight the enemy. Called Code Talkers, these skilled soldiers sent and received messages that could not be decoded by the Nazis or Imperial Japanese enemies. Which languages did they use? Choctaw, Navajo, Cherokee, Hopi, Osage, and more. The same languages that were forbidden in boarding schools and mainstream America, that were beaten out of young children. But those languages helped win two world wars.

The Code Talkers had first used their secret weapon in World War I. In one division, American Indian soldiers came from twenty-six different tribes, each with a different language or dialect. Some were assigned to work as messengers or telephone operators. They would send and receive important information in their individual languages to other members of their tribes at the battlefront. Those members then reported to their officers in English. When the Nazis tried to intercept the messages, they could not begin to translate the complicated American Indian dialects. One US commanding officer realized, "This is our code . . . it's unbreakable." Later, a captured German translator asked in frustration, "What language were they speaking?" His captors told him, "American."

Navajo Code Talkers Preston and Frank Toledo.

Further, during World War II, American Indians had served in white military units. Stateside they worked tirelessly beside white factory workers, welding tanks and sewing uniforms. As Code Talkers, they had implemented lifesaving codes. When the war was over, they wanted to continue in mainstream society. In addition, the war had changed the government's ability to protect Indian lands and funds. Money and assets had been redirected away from them for the war effort. Millions of acres of land had been carved out for factories, training camps, gunnery ranges, even incarceration camps for Japanese American families wrongly accused of siding with the enemy. The Council of Churches criticized Collier and the IRA for supporting Native American spiritual practices. After all, wasn't World War II about God and country?

Collier's vision for the government to help American Indians return to their lands and cultures slowly slipped away. It appeared that American Indian communities, the government, and mainstream society all wanted Indians to join the masses. At last, Collier admitted the inevitable. He would write, "Never before have they been so well prepared to take their places among the general citizenry and to become assimilated into the white population." In 1945, Collier resigned as commissioner of Indian Affairs. A new era of assimilation would begin. With it, boarding schools would reconsider American Indian education for the white world.

CHAPTER SIX

Hateful Things

In 2012 Andy Girty, who was teaching Cherokee language courses at Haskell Indian Nations University in Lawrence, Kansas, was given permission to make public a donation made to the Haskell Cultural Center and Museum. Girty gathered a few staff members and the journalist Mary Annette Pember, whom he had asked to come and record the event. Then he brought out a small quilt, carefully folded. As he unwrapped it, the room fell silent. Lying in the folds was a pair of tiny handcuffs, made of cold iron. Judging from the size, just a couple inches across, they were meant to fit a child perhaps five years old.

They had been donated by a white man named Shane Murray. Shane's grandfather had given him the handcuffs when Shane was eight or nine years old. He told Shane they were used to compel young Indian children to go to school. Shane must never play with them, his grandfather instructed him. Relatives later told Shane that his grandfather grew up in Oklahoma and had a grandmother who was Native American. No one knew her tribe, but perhaps the handcuffs had come from her. For the next

Tiny handcuffs that were used to restrain Native children.

thirty years, Shane guarded the handcuffs. But he always felt the burden of their secret. The handcuffs seemed alive to him. They seemed to move and hide from him for months at a time. Finally, they seemed to scream at Shane, *Take me home!* At last, around 2006, he brought them to Haskell Cultural Center and Museum and later said, "a huge weight had been lifted from my shoulders."

The question in everybody's mind was the same: *Why on God's earth would you want to handcuff a child of that age?* Was it to send a powerful message to the parents? Was it to tell the child that white adults are in complete power? Or was it simply for the psychological damage it would do to a parent or a grandparent as they watched their child handcuffed and taken away by force?

RECRUITING AT GUNPOINT

Clyde Blair, a white educator who rose from teacher to superintendent in the Indian boarding school system, worked at Haskell, Albuquerque, Carlisle, and Chilocco. As Albuquerque's principal, from 1910 to 1916, he provided details of his "recruiting" methods for Navajo students on "orders from Congress." Blair and a Navajo policeman traveled by horse-drawn buckboard from hogan to hogan (Navajo houses) looking for children. They heard parents shooing their children into the brush. They saw children darting every which way to escape. Halting the horses, the policeman stood up on the buckboard and fired his gun into the air. Then he jumped down and raced after the children. One at a time, he wrestled them to the ground and tied their hands and legs together. Then he and Blair lifted them onto the buckboard. Hog-tied, the children lay there as the superintendent and policeman traveled to the next village and the next, until their quota was filled.

To bring American Indians under white control, the US government took their children by force—if necessary, by the barrel of a gun. Then kept them in literal shackles. Did government agents convince themselves that these children were not humans at all but little animals? After a while, did the children's screams and cries even bother the agents? Or was it just another day's work?

All my personal experience comes from Chilocco Agricultural School and the stories from my family. My grandmother and mother shared only their good memories. They felt that the Quaker administrators were fair and that they both received good educations. But at the end of the day, Chilocco still followed strict rules set by the government, with the goal of wiping out American Indian culture. Beating and other forms of physical abuse were strictly forbidden at Chilocco. The administrators, however, found other ways to enforce their authority and make students follow rules to a T.

One way was to monitor students before each meal. Students had to march into the mess hall and line up at attention at their tables. That meant everyone looked straight ahead. If even one person tilted their head or moved their eyes, the entire student body had to stand for a full hour, without moving. If a child fainted, they were carried out, revived, then brought back to stand in line again. Then the unfortunate child received a demerit. If a student stacked up too many demerits, social and sports events and field trips were forbidden. The only way to work off demerits was through hard labor. Down on your hands and knees, you'd polish the floor or scrub the toilets or wash the basement floors for hours at a time.

Sometimes students were locked up. One student named Barbara, of the Cherokee and Pawnee Nations, attended Chilocco in the 1920s. She remembers being so homesick that all she wanted to do was escape. Finally, it was her birthday. The students were standing in line at attention, and Barbara took off running. The staff dragged her back and put her in lockup, a room with just a bed. Barbara was defiant. She kicked the slats out of the bed frame, so next, they took her shoes away. She stayed in lockup for two or three days until the matrons let her out.

Running away was a survival instinct, recalled Dennis Banks, who attended schools in Minnesota and the Dakotas. But getting caught meant the "hot line." Two lines of ten boys faced each other. Each boy held a stick, belt, or strap. The runaway ran between the lines and the boys struck him from all sides. In the 1960s and 1970s, Dennis Banks helped form the American Indian Movement for Native rights. He looked back in disbelief at his school days. "Can you imagine a government policy that encouraged kids to punish other kids?" he asked.

RUNAWAYS

Running away was an immediate instinct for so many boarding school students. They were deeply homesick. They were physically and emotionally harassed time and again. They missed their beloved traditions and ceremonies. Sometimes parents and relatives lived nearby and could signal that a ceremony was about to happen. They would send out drumbeats or light fires that glowed in the night. Children would slip away. Many knew their surroundings so well that they could hide in the landscape, evading any agents or police who were sent after them.

At Fort Stevenson School in the Dakotas, open from 1883 to 1894, Superintendent George W. Scott complained that the school was near a thick swamp and "all hope is lost" once runaways reached its tangled foliage. Runaways would be sought out by Indian agents, returned to school, and punished. Beatings, lockups in the school jail, or humiliation were possible. At Arizona's Fort Apache Indian School, Navajo male runaways returned in handcuffs. Then they were forced to wear girls' clothes for a week and march around the parade ground carrying heavy logs. Still, many students tried again. At Chilocco, 111 boys and 18 girls ran away during just four months in 1927. Another school lost one third of its students in one year, 1906–1907.

Some children were so desperate to go home that they never considered traveling conditions. One group of Yavapai boys walked a hundred miles through freezing rain and snow, without food or water, to escape Phoenix Indian School in Arizona. Young children might be too afraid to run away. They had heard of others getting lost or killed by wild animals. These things happened. But it was the "wee kindergarteners," wrote teacher Minnie Jenkins, who were the boldest runaways at Fort Mohave Indian School in Arizona. They succeeded so many times that they finally had to be locked up in the school prison. Then, one morning at breakfast, Minnie and the staff heard a repeated CRASH! BANG! CRUNCH! They raced to the prison. The big wooden door hung on its iron hinges. Beside it was a huge log. The free kindergarteners had found it outside and used it as a battering ram to break out their friends inside lockup. Looking out the window, the teachers saw the tiny "outlaws" running away, toward the riverbank.

Another kind of punishment was withholding the students' meager food rations, an effective way to hurt a child who never got enough food in the first place, even when that child was trying to be a good white person and a Christian. In the 1920s, the meals at Chilocco and other boarding schools were called "horrible . . . *terrible*" by one student. There were few fruits and vegetables, rarely a piece of meat. Noreen, a Potawatomi, remembered that sometimes there was stew with carrots and potatoes from the garden, but the vegetables were never fresh. For lunch they could often make their own sandwiches with bread baked in the Chilocco bakery. But the bread had no taste, and the students had only beans for filling. They would wolf down those sandwiches because there was nothing more. Sometimes there was a kind of cracker called hardtack. It was made with only flour and water. With luck, it contained salt. When you broke it open, worms popped out. Some students laughed about it later and said, "that's how we got extra protein." But at the time, when that student was hungry, it was horrifying. At other schools, dinner might be a potato, a small bit of meat, and coffee. Breakfast was cereal without milk. When milk was served, students might find a drowned mouse at the bottom of the pitcher.

One child in the Chamberlain, South Dakota, St. Joseph's Catholic Boarding School recalled being chosen to serve the priests their meals. While the children were fighting over their scanty share of food in the great hall, she walked into the priests' beautiful dining room. Their tables groaned with fresh fruits and vegetables, and with other delicacies, served on fancy plates with cups. "We used to stand there and look at it," said the student. "I would steal food whenever I could."

Holidays brought better meals at Chilocco, but you had to be on time, down to the second. Edgar, who was Cherokee, learned this the hard way in 1929. He loved Christmas dinner. The staff waited on the children. An orchestra played Christmas carols. A big meal was served, with meat and all the trimmings. The students could eat all they wanted. Edgar and his buddies had skipped breakfast so they could work up an appetite. They went out into the woods to hunt and pass the time. As the day went on, they listened for the bugle call. At last they heard it, and they raced toward the mess hall. But they were too far away. At precisely the last *ta-ta-ta-ta-ta-ta-da*, they arrived, just as the doors were being locked. The boys banged and shouted. No one would open the doors, even though it was Christmas Day. Edgar turned away and walked alone down to the school garden. He pulled up a couple of turnips. Then he built a fire and roasted them. "I could taste the salt because my tears were going down into every bite of the turnip," he said.

While "beating the Indian out" of children was not allowed at Chilocco, at other schools children were whipped, handcuffed, and chained to cellar walls. They were starved. Some children were sexually molested while teachers and principals turned their backs. In some boarding schools, abuse was routine. In those places, teachers dealt out physical punishment for the least broken rule. When the students first arrived, they were warned that they would be punished for a long list of violations. The worst punishments were meted out against cultural slips, such as speaking a single word of Native language. To keep children compliant, the staff and matrons might spread frightening rumors about what would happen if the students broke too many rules. One rumor was used in the early 1900s in religious institutions, especially those run by the Catholic church. The staff threatened that if a child could not be controlled, even after a series of small punishments, the child would be sent to a "hell on earth." Once you were sent there, you would never return. You would surely die there.

This place was called Hiawatha. That one word instilled fear in every boarding school student, from the youngest to the oldest. Hiawatha, in Canton, South Dakota, was the first and only federally funded psychiatric institution for American Indians in the US. Opened in 1903, it was operated by the United States government for thirty years. Among its horrors were the medical experiments with shock treatments and drug therapies practiced on the American Indian patients, including children. During the decades the institution was open, its staff inflicted lasting damage on members of many tribes. In 1933, the Bureau of Indian Affairs investigated reports that most patients were not mentally ill. When this was found to be true, Hiawatha was closed. The name Hiawatha was highly inappropriate. It was an insult to all American Indians because it was the name of the brilliant and respected leader of the Onondaga and Mohawk Nations of the Northeast, who lived in the 1700s. Among Chief Hiawatha's great achievements as a leader was to bring together the Iroquois Confederacy, an alliance of five Indian Nations that is still strong today.

Hiawatha Insane Asylum for Indians.

HIAWATHA INSANE ASYLUM FOR INDIANS

No boarding school student wanted to be sent to Hiawatha Insane Asylum for Indians. To punish inmates at Hiawatha, attendants wrapped them in straitjackets. These were then locked and chained to a bed for so long that the keys were often lost or their storage places forgotten. The stories from Hiawatha ran through all the tribal communities. It was said the stench was gagging. Many of the students who were sentenced to Hiawatha were simply "troublemakers." That is, they were kids who rebelled against unfair treatment. They might strike back at a matron when they were wrongly punished, a constant occurrence. When shackled to their beds, they might lie in their own feces for days. One girl with epilepsy was chained near a hot water pipe and barely missed being scalded during her seizures, miraculously escaping serious burns. Patients with disabilities might be sterilized so they could never have children. The so-called doctors were rarely qualified to administer such a procedure, and patients died. Some patients tried to run away. Others rebelled against the rat-infested food and horrifying conditions and incited riots among the patients in the dorms. Sadly, the most rebellious were forced to take a toxic drug called potassium bromide. At first it made patients lose all their energy. Over time, it caused hallucinations, making patients appear "insane."

Over half of the children sent to Hiawatha died and were buried there—at least 120 student names are documented on lists and grave markers. Many were children of tribal leaders who came from great leadership families such as the Lakota Chiefs Red Cloud and Standing Bear. Perhaps the government thought that sending high-born children to Hiawatha could control their families. Or perhaps a child who was damaged or dead could no longer carry on the tribal legacy.

A matron's or principal's threat to send a student to Hiawatha was a punishment in the extreme. Each boarding school had its own set of punishments that were dealt out swiftly and efficiently. Most left a lasting impression on the students. Staffs at Chemawa, Haskell, Pine Ridge, and Wahpeton worked hard to beat and shame children out of their culture. Rosalie Whirlwind Soldier, a member of the Lakota tribe in South Dakota, was only four years old when her mother died in the late 1940s. She was put into the St. Francis Indian School, part of the St. Francis Mission on the Rosebud Sioux Reservation near her home. Teachers told her that her Lakota language was "devil's speak." If she spoke Lakota or did not follow other rules, she was locked in the school basement. Sometimes she was there for weeks. The experience still haunted Rosalie as she told her story in 2022 when she was seventy-eight years old. Another constant reminder of her days at boarding school was her bad leg. She walked with a limp because she broke her leg in an accident. The doctors were careless in setting it, and it never healed properly.

A young Kiowa student named Myrtle Ware went to Rainy Mountain Boarding School in Oklahoma, from 1898 to 1907. The school stood in the shadow of her people's sacred mountain, Sepyalda. Its first white superintendent, Cora Dunn, wrote to the US commissioner of Indian Affairs that "our purpose is to change [Indian children] forever." Myrtle learned to watch out for one matron who "goes around and listens." If the matron caught students speaking Kiowa, she gave them demerits so they could not go to events and outings. Other matrons were harsher. They forced students to brush their teeth with soapy toothbrushes. One girl remembered having to hold bitter quinine tablets in her mouth. Quinine tablets were used for treating malaria but were harmful if you weren't sick. Others had to carry stepladders on their shoulders for hours at a time. Humiliation was another tactic. One boy was sent to the laundry room to join the girls working there. He had to wear an apron and wash socks for two days.

Like punishments for speaking their tribal language, children suffered other punishments for doing anything culturally or tribally related. There were punishments for dancing, for praying, for telling stories, for braiding their hair. The long list of "offenses" included Indian gestures. There is a facial expression common among tribes throughout Indian country, which is pointing with your lips. If someone asks you for directions to a place, you simply pucker your lips slightly and point in the direction the person wishes to go. Then you go back to what you were doing. Each different Indian culture has its own way to make this directional gesture. Some gestures are eloquent, a slight and very beautiful motion. Others give a more pronounced version, perhaps pursing your lips more distinctly or also nodding your head. We are raised with these gestures from the time we are born. They are cultural characteristics, and we do them without thinking. But in a boarding school, that little expression could earn you some serious licks with a belt or a strap or a rod or a paddle.

Certain disciplinarians kept a collection of tools to inflict various levels of pain, depending on the infraction. Some of these techniques dated back to the Inquisition, an institution in medieval Europe where people were punished and sometimes executed for not believing in the Catholic faith. A horsewhip might hang on a wall to indicate to a child, "Look what God has in store for you if you don't obey!" A razor strap, ruler, or belt might be stored in a box in a desk drawer. When the drawer was pulled out, students would know that a whipping was coming— or worse. When St. Margaret's Indian Residential School in Ontario, Canada, was being torn down in the 1970s, a former student rummaged through artifacts before they were thrown away. He stopped cold. There was the strap once used to beat him. More than a foot wide, it was made of heavy canvas from a conveyor belt. Its worn handle was wrapped with black tape. The tip of the strap was stained with the dried blood of many children.

The story of Matthew War Bonnet, a Lakota who was sent to St. Francis Indian School in South Dakota in the 1940s, is chilling. Matthew told a reporter from the *Everett Herald*, in Washington State, that the Catholic priests who ran the school had a favorite tool for punishment. They called it the Jesus Rope. This heavy rope was braided into a three-foot cord. Each time a child was beaten, large welts rose across their little body. Matthew was just six years old when he received his first beating. He remembered that the rope had been used to whip so many other children that it was frayed, with broken strands. One priest used a razor strap. Another, a cattle prod. Worse still, the children who were abused became so angry that they abused other students. That behavior continued after they grew up, married, and raised their own families.

John Campbell, an Elder in Washington State's Tulalip Tribes, had always wondered why his father grew agitated when John used poor table manners. John later learned that matrons at Chemawa, his father's school, would stab a child's hand with a fork if the child reached across the table for food. As with Denise K. Lajimodiere's parents, Teri Gobin, chairwoman of the Tulalip Tribes, said that her father had trouble saying the words *I love you*. He had never heard those words spoken at school. Matthew War Bonnet remembered taking out his own anger on his family. In his late seventies, he still had recurring nightmares about those days.

So did Harriette Shelton Dover. As a little girl of seven years old in 1911, she was sent to Tulalip Indian School in Washington State. Like so many other children, she sometimes slipped into speaking her Snohomish dialect of the Coast Salish language. One time, a matron overheard her. Furious, the matron grabbed Harriette and thrashed her with a horsewhip from her neck to her ankles. Harriette never forgot the incredible pain and the horror as each blow rained down. And she never forgot the look on the matron's face as she struck harder and harder. Years later, Harriette discovered that the same kind of horsewhip was banned by state penitentiaries because it was too brutal to use on hardened criminals. But they used it on us, she remembered. "What did we do? We were nine years old, and we were speaking our language."

The stories of children who were punished for simply being children are endless. Nuns and priests and other administrators said the children had to learn to "obey." Those people in power gave children scars that lasted all their lives, some physical, some psychological. Around 1930, little Donald Kolchakis was just eight years old when the priest at St. Boniface Indian Industrial Boarding School in California insisted he join the band. Donald said he didn't want to join the band. Instead of helping Donald find another activity to join, the priest, Father Justin, whipped him "for impudence." Other children who were homesick and frightened often wet their beds. Instead of helping the child, a matron might whack the student with a paddle (sometime called the board of education), or rub the student's face in the urine or order them to display the soaked sheet above the bed.

Indian children sometimes wanted to go to boarding school to escape family problems at home. Soon, however, they found that things were worse. Cecelia (not her real name) was a member of the Sisseton Wahpeton Oyate tribe in South Dakota, and things at home were bad. Cecelia's father was an alcoholic. Her mother beat her with a strap until she broke out in welts. Her grandfather sexually molested her. The moment Cecelia arrived at Wahpeton Indian School in North Dakota, she realized things were deeply wrong. As she walked to the school entrance, a girl on a swing accidentally got her feet wet in a puddle. A matron grabbed the girl and horsewhipped her until her back and legs bled. As Cecelia settled into school, another matron took a dislike to her. Each time she saw Cecelia, she nagged her and slapped her in the head. The little girl finally collapsed in fear and pain. For three months she lay in the infirmary, unable to feed herself or even get out of bed without her legs crumpling beneath her. Later, she refused to talk about it.

RUNNING THE GAUNTLET

Corporal punishment is one of the most extreme physical punishments a person can receive. The US government told boarding schools they could use it only in cases of "grave violation." But that rule was stretched. Leo Lajimodiere learned how much. He once mentioned to a friend that he thought the headmaster and dorm matron "liked each other." Another boy overheard him and reported him. For this simple bit of gossip, Leo's punishment was to "run the gauntlet."

That term struck fear into every student. Every school had a different kind of gauntlet, but each one meant unbearable beatings and pain. At Chemawa, Leo was ordered to lie face down on a bed. Then two boys held his arms and legs as all the other boys lined up behind him. The first boy in line was handed a strap with metal studs. He was told to hit Leo as hard as he could across the back, buttocks, and legs. Then he passed the strap to the next boy. If any boy struck Leo too gently, he was forced to take Leo's place. One after another, the boys hit Leo as hard as they could, until his back was ripped and bleeding. Leo passed out and woke up in the infirmary. He stayed there for two weeks. Leo's physical scars eventually healed, but his emotional scars never did. Leo was fortunate. A Browning Blackfeet boy died during the gauntlet when his kidneys ruptured.

The most lasting horror against children was sexual abuse. It ran rampant in all schools, whether administrators were government employees or Christian clerics. Julia, who had attended St. Joseph's Catholic Boarding School in Chamberlain, North Dakota, today lives on the Turtle Mountain Reservation in the state. She told Denise K. Lajimodiere that her nightmare started out as her happiest day at the school. A priest was having a birthday, and Julia was excited because she was chosen to go to his party. She was just five years old and the smallest girl in the school, so she felt very special. The nuns put together a big gift box, and Julia and another classmate, a little boy, climbed inside. At just the right moment, they jumped out and sang "Happy Birthday." The priest was delighted, and everyone laughed. The day was a big success for Julia. Soon after that, however, the priest began calling Julia out of class. She told the nuns she didn't want to go, but they insisted. She would go to the priest's chamber, and he would lock his door. Then he would sexually molest her. If another member of the staff knocked unexpectedly, he would shut Julia in the closet so no one knew. Julia was afraid to tell anyone. After a few years she finally left the school, but she never forgot that time. Later, she said she could not be in a small space because it reminded her of the closet. To this day, she will not shake the hand of a priest.

At every school, the students were forced to work, work, work. Despite long days of marching, attending classes, cleaning the dorms, and doing homework, the children were forced to do manual labor. The boys built dormitories and high walls and gymnasiums. They paved roads. They dug wells. They made chairs and desks. They plowed the fields and tended crops. The girls cleaned dormitories and bathrooms, washed clothes, picked fruit, harvested crops, milked cows, and processed the milk to make butter and cheese. Students who broke rules could suddenly find themselves doing hours of extra labor. At St. Boniface, being late, talking back, or other disobedience could mean spending the afternoon loading and pushing wheelbarrows of dirt to a new construction site, pouring concrete, or polishing floors for hours on hands and knees.

Sometimes students fought back. In the 1920s, Martha Manuel Chacon, of California's San Manuel Band of Mission Indians, was always in trouble at St. Boniface. During daily duties in the laundry room, the nuns assigned her to wash the dirty underwear. One day, Martha had had enough of underwear. She decided to wash the jeans instead. When a nun told Martha to stop, Martha ignored her. The nun slapped Martha. Martha slapped her back, in the face. The nun screamed that Martha had sinned because she had slapped an agent of God. Martha told the nun *she* had sinned because she had slapped an Indian. The nun ran to complain. Soon Martha was dragged away and whipped by the priest on duty, Father Justin, the same priest who had beaten Donald Kolchakis for not wanting to join the band. When the next holiday arrived, Martha went home and begged her parents to enroll her in the local school. She told them she refused to return to St. Boniface because children were treated like slaves.

Besides working at the school, older students might be trained to work in the community as part of an experiment called the outing program. Richard Henry Pratt had started the outing program at Carlisle Industrial School so the students could live with white families and learn more about lifestyles in the community. It was another way to further alienate students from their families, by keeping them away from home year-round. They would use the English language, practice white manners, and work in jobs that required the skills they had learned at school. Boys worked as carpenters and farmers, girls as nannies and housekeepers. It was just one more step to fully remove students from their culture and make them complete members of white society. Pratt monitored the Carlisle program with an eagle eye. Students reported being happy. Families reported good relationships. Pratt believed it was a success. But students rarely told the true story, for fear of punishment. In actuality, the outing program led to a wider form of abuse.

Carlisle set an example for other boarding schools to start outing programs, and many of those programs turned dark. At the Sherman Institute in California, it was a way for locals to get cheap field labor. Boys from the Navajo and Hopi tribes worked for a big farming corporation. The managers couldn't care less about giving the boys a valuable experience. In fields under the blazing sun, the students worked ten-hour days. Instead of living with a family, they were packed into shacks buzzing with flies and filled with foul odors from the overflowing latrines. Some girls had better experiences because they worked inside family homes. But school administrators didn't keep careful watch. Girls also worked long hours cleaning, cooking, and caring for children. Rarely were the backgrounds of the host families checked. Many young women were sexually molested by their male employers.

A letter written in 1952 shows the lack of care for a child's safety. It is written by the Tekakwitha Indian Mission administrator to a couple in South Dakota. The administrator thanks

A thank-you note from Father John Pohlen for the $10 donation for the adoption of Dennis Isaac Seely by a couple in Illiniois.

the couple for their "donation of 10.00 for my little Indians." For that price, the administrator will "send a little boy of six or older, or a little girl, whatever you prefer." It ends with the chilling words, "I am not making any inquiries about you because it takes a good person to make an offer as you did." Many such "good" people on the surface turned out to be far from that.

Punishments passed from generation to generation. Children who had learned abusive ways at boarding school used them on their own children, as happened with John Campbell, Teri Gobin, and Denise K. Lajimodiere. Denise never attended a boarding school, but she remembers her mother using the same discipline that matrons used. If Denise and her sister were disobedient, her mother would send them to kneel in a corner as punishment. Denise was thankful that she never had to kneel on a broomstick, the punishment for so many children. Her father's discipline was harsher. He would whip them with his belt. During her research on American Indian boarding schools and interviewing survivors, Denise came to understand why her parents parented her and her siblings the way they did. It's because they had learned how from the unkind and often vicious nuns, priests, and other administrators who "parented" them. This gut-wrenching pattern was handed down through generations in countless American Indian families.

As with other improvements to boarding schools, the Meriam Report and John Collier's tenure in the Bureau of Indian Affairs led to many schools being reprimanded or closed for harmful behavior toward children. Such treatment persisted as other schools remained open until 1980. For years, many survivors kept their stories locked away, deep inside themselves. They had been told they were worthless. They were dirty. They could not be educated. They felt shame. Even as they progressed and succeeded in life, those feelings remained. One day, the world would hear their stories.

At all schools everywhere, Indian students were indoctrinated in white ways. But, in a twist of fate, boarding schools helped revive and reinforce tribes. By bringing together children of many Indian Nations, the schools promoted cultural sharing that might not otherwise have happened. Children of strong tribal traditions willingly shared with children whose tribes had been driven to the edge of existence. Gradually, those endangered cultures were restored and strengthened. A Pan-Indian culture of solidarity and sharing developed across the nation. Today's intertribal powwows are an example of that culture. They underscore the power of working together, while remaining unique.

Children everywhere found ways to honor and share their cultures, weaving their practices quietly into the white routine. Sometimes they even had fun. At South Dakota's Holy Rosary Mission School in Pine Ridge, a group of Lakota girls collected discarded scraps of material from the sewing room and food and boxes from the kitchen. During playtime, they retreated to a corner of the playground and set up doll camps, with two-feet-tall tepees of sticks and muslin, wagons made of cereal boxes, and dolls with beaded eyes and hair cut from their own. A tiny dog and horse molded from discarded gumbo soup and dried in the sun would watch over the camp. Such Native-inspired behavior might have been squelched. But the town residents enjoyed watching through the fences, praising the school for the well-behaved and creative children they had "trained" so successfully. Children at Rainy Mountain Boarding School used their Native skills to snare a menagerie of possums and raccoons for a circus. Gathering materials from trash heaps, they fashioned drums and other musical instruments and a "sculpture" of a buffalo. Then they performed acrobatics and sideshows to amuse the teachers, demonstrating the athletics and other skills they'd learned.

Francis La Flesche of the Omaha Nation looked up to a band of boys called the Big Seven at Presbyterian Mission School in Bellevue, Nebraska, in the 1870s. They quietly but firmly guarded their heritage. One day a group of white visitors asked the boys if they knew any "Indian songs." After a moment, one of the Big Seven belted out a few chords of a tribal victory song. Then the entire student body joined in with such force and emotion that the visitors went slack-jawed. The boys were secretly proud. After that, they had to attend daily classes to learn "civilized" white hymns and ballads. But, Francis recalled, for one brief moment they had the "thrill of connecting with the deep cultural stirrings" of their Omaha tradition. Francis La Flesche became a keeper of the Omaha tradition. In 1879, the Smithsonian Institution founded its Bureau of American Ethnology to hold the stories of all American Indians. Francis had become an anthropologist and was named the first American Indian staff member. His book, *The Middle Five: Indian Schoolboys of the Omaha Tribe*, published in 1900, tells some hilarious, and tragically true, stories of his boarding school days.

At night in the dark dormitories, after matrons were fast asleep, the children would come alive. They'd plan pranks or ways to make it home for a tribal dance, or ways to leave forever. At Chilocco, they'd sneak to the woods to roast corn over campfires or hold all-night stomp dances. Inside the dorm, stories would keep children talking through the night. One Mescalero Apache boy from New Mexico recalled telling tales of the mythical troublemaker Coyote. Listeners "would break out laughing" at the end. Girls at Phoenix, in Arizona, learned to mimic the matrons they detested most. One they nicknamed Ho'ok after the legendary Pima witch. The imitator strung nails together to sound like jingling keys. Walking among the beds at night she'd wheeze in a nasally voice, "Girls! Girls!" Little ones screeched and scattered. The night ended in giggles.

Most important, children found ways to keep the language. It was their heritage, and it was sacred. At Rainy Mountain, two young students were able to pass love letters back and forth in Kiowa. To escape punishment if they were caught using their own language, they used the white man's alphabet to spell out Kiowa phrases. The words did not make sense in English, but that didn't matter. They had followed the rules. Those students later married. The love letters of Parker McKenzie and Nettie Odelty became the basis for the Kiowa written language today. Rainy Mountain Boarding School now lies in ruins, but the sacred mountain Sepyalda still towers silently above the rubble, perhaps a sign that the Kiowa heritage has outlived the white man's influence.

CHAPTER SEVEN

Changes in the 1950s

In my grandmother's and mother's time at Chilocco, the students would complain about not getting enough to eat, especially the young boys. My brother Mike told me the small boys learned to spit in their milk so the big boys wouldn't take it from them. Parish Williams, whom I called uncle, graduated from Chilocco in 1932. He once told me they would get so hungry that they would sneak out at night and go down to the creek. There they would cut long, straight willow limbs and sharpen one end. They would make their way to the root cellars below the storage space for the agricultural equipment. These root cellars were cut into the earth, lined with concrete, then covered with more earth. Only the door was exposed. Half a dozen of these caves stood side by side, in a row. Each contained a different kind of crop to keep warm in winter and cool in the summer. Before refrigeration, root cellars were how people stored food. It was the apples the boys wanted.

The doors were made of thick solid wood and were always locked. But all the doors had windows covered with metal bars. Guiding their long willow spears between those bars, the boys could spear apples. They would poke one apple at a time and bring it out through the window. They would gather as many apples as they could, then they'd make off to a secret place to enjoy them. Once the boys got their fill of apples, the remaining ones made great items to trade with the other boys. You didn't need money. With apples you could buy someone's time to shine your shoes, clean your room, and do other mundane tasks. As for a girl who wanted an apple, a boy might trade one for the girl's company on a kind of "date." It was called night-hawking. A boy would coordinate a rendezvous with a young lady to meet in a secret place. They'd spend the evening talking and hanging out. Many future marriages came out of night-hawking.

HUNGRY

Students at Indian boarding schools were always hungry. It did not help that they had to adjust to white man's food. Even if they would eat it, there was never enough. The US government regulations in the Department of the Interior's 1890 report read that "Good and healthful provisions must be supplied in abundance; and they must be well cooked . . ." But that was far from the reality.

One student at Chamberlain Indian School recalled breakfast. A box of cereal was set on the table and passed around. If you were the last to get it, nothing was left. The same went for the pitcher of milk. In other schools, food was set in the center of the table and the biggest students grabbed it first, leaving nothing for the younger, slower students. "I learned very quickly, if you wanted to eat you had to be fast," wrote Curtis T. Carr, a student at Chilocco. Curtis finally discovered that he could be a waiter. With the other boys who waited dinner tables, he went early to the cafeteria. He was given dinner before anyone else. One little boy at Chilocco was simply helped by two older boys who felt sorry for him. The big boys stole bread from the bakery and honey from the beehives to feed him. Sadly, stealing was the solution for many starving kids. But being caught meant suffering the consequences. When Dennis Decoteau was a student at Wahpeton School in North Dakota, like many others, he was always hungry. One day he took a bottle of cherries from the cafeteria. The next thing he knew, he was kneeling on a broomstick. Then a priest ordered him to pull down his pants, and the priest beat him with a fiberglass fishing rod.

As we've seen, some positive changes started to take place at the boarding schools under John Collier's direction at the IBA and the passage of the Indian Reorganization Act. By the time my elder sister Donna Jones began school at Chilocco in 1953, she could take advantage of those many positive changes. She majored in two vocational courses: journalism and home economics. Like our grandmother and mother before her, after she graduated in 1957 she got a job at Chilocco as an employee. Donna said Grandmother Elizabeth was her primary influence in attending Chilocco. But she also had another role model: Aunt Otilia, Velma's younger sister. Known as Tillie to her friends and family, she had excelled at Chilocco and later served as a Bureau of Indian Affairs executive assistant at the school until it closed.

Otilia "Tillie" Hernandez during her Chilocco years.

Thanks especially to Collier's IRA, by that time it was not forced attendance. Indian children of grade school or high school age went to Chilocco because they wanted to go. Many wanted to leave unhappy homes. Most went for the education they would receive. In reality, Chilocco lagged behind non-Indian public schools in academic education. But its vocational training meant students could get real employment after they graduated.

The switch to vocational training was an important one made by L. E. Correll, who became superintendent of the school during Donna's time there. While Correll supported new opportunities and the return of heritage for students, he had disagreed with the Meriam Report's outlook on academic versus vocational courses. A graduate of Oklahoma State University, a school that focused on agricultural training, Correll saw the benefit of teaching students hands-on skills for finding good jobs. During his administration he instituted no fewer than forty-five vocational courses in agricultural training alone. That was somewhat of a record among the Indian schools. Every student who knew Correll had only good things to say about him. It was said that he knew each student by their name, even when the school enrollment reached one thousand. He made himself accessible to the students. He honestly wanted to know what they thought about their education. Even more, he stopped the harsh punishments. My sister had witnessed both periods, with and without the punishments. She said the school was much

L. E. Correll.

better without them. During this time, our aunt Tillie was there as well, working as an executive assistant. She set an example for young women, like her niece Donna, to strive for success and independence.

But my sister never had trouble at Chilocco. She followed the rules and she was bright. She earned straight A's the entire time. Even after she graduated and took a job at the school, she continued studying, taking advantage of the rich curriculum. Donna worked for Correll in his office. It was a job she really enjoyed—and she was paid for it! It seems obvious to expect to get paid for work, but it was the first job at Chilocco for which a student was paid. Correll soon instituted salaries for all the working students, a new experience for them. Donna was able to buy clothing for the office and for special occasions. And she saved money for her future. She loved studying current events in her journalism classes as well as interviewing people and learning about their lives. But girls were never encouraged to pursue careers such as journalism. It was home economics she had to take more seriously.

It was typical that Chilocco would prepare the young girls for a married life after school, as did nearly all schools across America during this time. Donna was expected to make use of homemaking skills as a wife and mother. Home economics classes included sewing, cooking, baking, entertaining, and health. At one point, Donna had a home ec course called Cottage Living. It was an all-inclusive course on living as a wife and mother after graduation. On one part of the campus was a group of small houses. The female students would be assigned to a cottage, then they'd set it up as a home. They'd even live there for a few weeks. Some Chilocco employees would bring their children for the girls to take care of during the day. Instructors would arrive in the morning and teach them to cook, clean, and care for the little ones. The lessons served Donna well. She married soon after she left Chilocco, and she raised a family. Later, she used her journalism training and became a poet as well as an artist in the Ponca community.

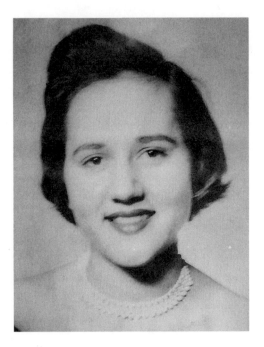

Donna Jones during her Chilocco years.

Although Donna's story at Chilocco is a personal success story, in other ways it is sad for the bigger Ponca story. It shows that the boarding school program worked just as the government intended. Donna and her Chilocco community had learned to follow white ways. They spoke primarily English. Still, Donna never lost the strength of her Ponca spirit. She continued passing down Ponca stories to her children. She remained deeply committed to her family and her community. Until she passed away in 2023, she remained a respected member of the Ponca tribe, bringing knowledge and wisdom to us all.

STRONG WOMEN

"A woman's place is in the home" was the rule in white American society in the early 1900s. White women were seen as delicate flowers who needed stronger people to make a living for them. Those people included men, as well as African American and American Indian women. A male speaker at the 1893 National Congress of Mothers announced that these "other" women could endure "effort, exposure, and hardship." American Indian boarding schools bought into that idea. They prepared female students to be servants who could work in white people's homes and respect their authority. If a white girl wanted to break the mold, she could go to school to become a teacher, nurse, or businesswoman. An American Indian girl had a narrower choice. Her school was in the laundry room, the kitchen, and the sewing room. Most female graduates later used their skills to raise families or to work as domestic help. Others sought greater opportunity.

In the late 1800s, Susan La Flesche Picotte's father enrolled her in the white-run Quaker mission school on her Omaha Reservation in Nebraska, and she later taught there. A natural healer, she often nursed people back to health, including a white anthropologist working with her tribe named Alice Fletcher. Alice encouraged Susan to attend medical school, and Susan went east to Virginia's Hampton Institute and the Women's Medical College of Pennsylvania. Susan soon became the first Native American woman to earn a medical degree. On her reservation she later opened the first Native American hospital without government help. Named Walthill Hospital, it is known today as Dr. Susan La Flesche Picotte Memorial Hospital.

Later, my own mother became a brilliant entrepreneur who started a restaurant and used her language skills to help her Ponca community. My sister Donna was a successful artist whose paintings have been exhibited country-wide. Still later, in the 1970s and 1980s, Cherokee member Wilma Mankiller continued opening doors for Native women. As a young girl, she and her family lived through a traumatic government relocation from Oklahoma to San Francisco. There, Wilma struggled in a local white high school. But she followed her parents' advice to never let anyone define her, that she must define herself. Wilma became an activist for her people and rose to become the first female Principal Chief of the Cherokee Nation. For her extraordinary advancements in education, jobs, and health care for her people, she was awarded the Medal of Freedom by President Bill Clinton. These women and others like them inspire young American Indian women today to reach for the stars.

Velma Pensoneau Jones (left) with longtime friend Wilma Mankiller (right).

While Donna's story is mostly a happy one, her road was not completely smooth. As with most other Indian families, situations at home made them sad or worried or sent them into depression. Some students had parents who were alcoholics or living in extreme poverty. Some had younger siblings who lived with abusive relatives. The family harmony that had existed among tribes for thousands of years was shattered within a century as white people stole our lands and pushed us from our homes. American history books praise the opportunities the West offered white pioneers. But the books don't tell how our Indian families and communities were destroyed. We no longer had control over our lives or our futures or the pride of making our living from the bounty of nature. We were crowded into small reservations, pushed into white men's houses and schools. We were told to live by white men's rules. We were forced to work in their factories and businesses. The result was crushing. We could not be ourselves. We could not flourish. Reservations became areas of profound poverty. Many lost their sense of purpose. Tempers were short. Arguments were frequent. Young people with bright futures lost their way. Many died of illness or from fighting among themselves. Every household felt it. Our household felt the loss of our brother Warren Jones.

Even though Warren was actually a first cousin to Donna and me, in the Ponca tradition he *was* our brother. I was just a baby at the time, but Donna was close in age to Warren. She looked up to him. Everyone looked up to Warren. He was quite the man. Some people would call him "a man's man." He was a champion rodeo athlete who won many awards in competitions such as bull and bronco riding and roping and steer wrestling. Warren was tough as nails. The family liked to say, "He covered all the ground he walked on." One night, Warren got into a fight with another man over the man's estranged wife. Later, Warren didn't want any hard feelings. He wanted to clear the air and shake hands. So, he went to find the man to settle things. As Warren entered a darkened room, the man stepped from the shadows and shot Warren in the face with a shotgun. He killed our big brother Warren.

Donna and the whole family took Warren's death extremely hard. For months it was difficult for Donna to study and work in the superintendent's office while mourning her older brother. He, like many other young men, was a casualty of the white plan to change us. Every person at Chilocco had his or her own family grief, and some could not survive it. Donna was one of the strong ones. She persevered and gave strength to others.

Besides the loss of Warren back at home, Donna told me the saddest time as a student that she can remember at the school was the day she saw a Navajo boy crying. He was very young, only five or six years old. It was the 1950s, and most tribes were used to sending their children to boarding schools. Not the Navajo Nation. Navajo parents wanted their children to stay at home, to fully keep their language and traditions. What's more, this child had been stolen from his parents at an age far younger than was advised by the Meriam Report. Donna saw an older Navajo boy trying to console the child. The child didn't speak English, and the older boy didn't speak much English, either.

Donna asked the older boy what was wrong with the child. The older boy turned to her and said, "Mother, he misses." Donna told me her eyes welled up. She felt helpless. That little boy's grief really impacted her. She recalled the stories of her own grandmother being torn from her parents. Why would such young children be taken away from their parents and so far away from their loved ones?

In 1954, about the time Donna was adjusting to losing Warren, our brother Dennis Michael Jones showed up at Chilocco. Mike, as he was known, was tall and lean. He had suffered from asthma for his entire life, and Donna felt responsible for his health while he was at the school. Mike had to be careful because something as minor as a common cold could endanger his ability to breathe. But this didn't slow him down much. Mike was determined to be as active as the rest of his classmates. He went out for track and field. He enrolled in the agricultural vocation classes to do heavy manual work on the farm. Soon he was pulling long hours like the other boys.

One of the stories Mike told was about working with the Chilocco mules. The school had a log barn with a couple dozen of the animals. Mules are said to be stronger than horses and

My brother Dennis Michael "Mike" Jones.

much smarter. If you were trying to work with a disgruntled mule, you had better just hang it up because the mule would win every time. The boys who worked with the mules had a special prank they would pull on new boys assigned to the mule barn. Each mule worked for six days a week, then was given one day off. Every mule's day off was different, and every mule knew its own day. When a new boy came on, the older boys would assign him to a mule on its day off. As hard as the new boy tried, he could not get that mule to budge!

Mike soon found out that hauling hay gives off too much dust and requires too much hard lifting for someone with asthma. He started feeling the stress of farmwork, and he had trouble breathing. Thanks to Superintendent Correll's new rules, he could transfer to a less strenuous vocation. There was a wide range to choose from: printing, baking, power plant operation, masonry, food prep, dry cleaning, foundry (iron works), shoe repair, auto mechanics, dairy operations, leather crafts, carpentry, electricity, blacksmith, welding, cosmetology, animal husbandry, and home economics. He could work at one of those trades for half the day. Then he would pursue his academic courses for the other half. Those included math, science, English, geography, and history.

But whatever his vocational training, Mike was always in danger of grave illness while at Chilocco. It didn't help that the activities never stopped or slowed down. Keeping the kids active was one of the goals of the administration, even if a kid like Mike had a life-threatening disease. Because of constant exertion, he suffered many severe asthma attacks where he could barely breathe. Any one of them could have ended his life. Mike faced other dangers, too. In the close quarters at Chilocco he was vulnerable to communicable diseases such as influenza, measles, and mumps that easily spread from student to student. One day, Mike felt very ill. He could breathe just fine, so he knew he wasn't having an asthma attack. But the overall sick feeling wouldn't go away.

Finally, Mike went to see the nurse on duty. She gave him a thorough physical and told him, "You have the mumps!" At that time, there was no vaccine yet and mumps could be a serious disease. Like a cold, it was a virus that spread by coughing

Mike (right) and me (left).

or sneezing—and it was extremely contagious. The nurse was about to send Mike back to his dorm, where he could have infected every boy there. Donna came to the rescue. She had studied mumps in some of her classes, and she knew how dangerous the disease was. She made the nurse promise to keep Mike in a room alone. Donna's intervention helped Mike get better. And it quite possibly saved Chilocco from an epidemic.

In general, Donna and Mike felt their years at Chilocco were good ones. Our sister Charmain entered Chilocco in 1958 and Esther in the 1960s. By then, both Donna and Mike had graduated but were working there. While Esther stayed only a short while before transferring to the local public high school, Charmain flourished at Chilocco. She enjoyed the benefits of older siblings watching out for her and the positive changes happening at Chilocco. Overall, boarding schools were easing strict rules and welcoming Native practices. Opportunities opened up for students. One proactive club was Chilocco's Indian Club. It brought together members of many different tribes. Guided by a trained researcher, the students helped one another delve into their cultures and identify their traditional dress. Some students had never worn their regalia at home. Photographs from the 1950s and 1960s Chilocco yearbooks show students dressed in full regalia for gatherings or parades, as well as those in western clothing working in vocational classrooms. Chilocco was setting a stage for students to reclaim their

Marie Brown and Gordon Roy, Chilocco Princess
and Chilocco Brave, 1957.

heritage and pride, and to spread that pride through their communities while learning to work in white society.

But there were still reminders of the traditional boarding school meanness and discipline that ruined the best of days. After Mike graduated from Chilocco, he continued to live and work there as part of the night staff. During the day he attended nearby Arkansas Junior College in Arkansas City, Kansas. Then, after school, he worked part time as a printer for the local newspaper. When that work ended at five p.m., he would run as fast as he could the five miles back to Chilocco. Every day, in every kind of weather. He had to beat the closing of the cafeteria doors at six p.m if he wanted dinner. It was always a close call. Many times, as he ran through the campus gates, he would see the cafeteria staff closing the doors in the distance, then locking them. They clearly saw Mike, too. And they saw that he was running. They must have known he was looking forward to dinner after a long day. All Mike could do was watch them lock the doors. Then he would go home hungry. But Mike persevered. He was successful after his Chilocco years. He later worked for a company that used 3M products to print books and magazines. In 1969 he was honored as the 3M Printer of the Year.

Leupp Hall, cafeteria at Chilocco.

HEALING HUMOR

There were hard times at Chilocco. But there was also humor, and lots of funny people. Humor is the one thing that has helped Indians cope with demoralization and depression. Almost all tribes have their jokers and pranksters, much like the mythical character Coyote. Coyote breaks the rules and gets in trouble, but he entertains and often teaches lessons through his misadventures.

Our Coyotes were Archie Little Walker and his brother, Newman, who worked at Chilocco with Donna. They were members of the Kaw tribe related to the Ponca. They were relentless. But, man, were they funny! It was even funnier when the tables turned on them. One autumn, it was time for leaf cleanup on the Chilocco campus with its many, many trees. Archie's job was to drive the tractor from pile to pile of leaves until his trailer was filled, then dump the load off campus. On this day, someone had been careless with a cigarette. The mass of leaves in Archie's trailer started to smolder. No one noticed until Archie was on his way to the dump, with the full load engulfed in flames! A stiff wind was blowing, so he drove along, oblivious to the crackling fire and the smell as smoke spewed out of the trailer. Soon he noticed people waving and pointing along his route. Archie naturally thought what a popular guy he was. He began waving back! Then he was doing the princess wave. He doffed his shabby baseball cap as if it were a big Stetson cowboy hat and nodded proudly. His smile stretched from ear to ear. The crowd was frantic.

Fortunately, he soon passed the local fire department. Firemen rushed to douse the flames before Archie could go much farther. But Archie never missed a beat. He jumped from the tractor and bowed to the crowds as if he had saved the day. Just like Coyote. Archie Little Walker, you were meant to be there. You helped everyone prepare for just about anything life threw at us!

Beyond the boarding schools, the 1950s were a time of change for all Indian Nations. The earlier Meriam Report and then the Indian Reorganization Act had tried to stop the further loss of Indian lands by blocking the government from selling them. The IRA was intended to restore financial aid. But in the early

1940s, World War II budgets eliminated funds that could have supported the program. As the 1950s loomed, legislators complained that Collier's policy would forever keep Indians under government control and would cost the American public too much money. Besides, they said, many Indians were complaining about the IRA. Indians who had successfully joined white society called the IRA a "back to the blanket" policy, meaning backward. Many were abandoning reservation life for the city.

In 1946, the US Congress under President Harry Truman reiterated that Indians should become part of mainstream society. Truman approved the Indian Claims Commission. It would pay Indian tribes a fee for the lands they claimed the United States had stolen. But the lands would not be returned. This was a blow. Indians' ancestral territories were lost to them forever. On top of that, in 1948, a new Bureau of Indian Affairs commissioner, William Brophy, set another policy. Indians would be relocated to cities. Tribal communities would once again be shattered.

As a final blow, in 1953, Congress supported a resolution that would become known as the Termination Policy. It was an experiment with a handful of tribes. The plan was to dissolve reservations and give the same "privileges and responsibilities" to Indians as other US citizens had. It would break all the previous treaties the United States had made with tribes to protect them and give them financial aid. Tribes would no longer be recognized as their own sovereign, or independent, ruling entities.

Washington lawmakers held that the policy gave Indians the freedom and opportunity to be like everyone else in America. If the experiment worked, all tribes would come under the policy. From our perspective, it was a stab in the back. As one Blackfeet tribal chairman said, "The only translation in our language for 'termination' is 'to wipe out' or 'kill off.'"

Some American Indians did thrive in the cities. Many others were out of their element. They found the life impossible. They had never dealt with traffic lights, telephones, lack of housing, or even taking an elevator. They faced prejudice. Alcoholism rose. Many wanted to return to reservations, but they no longer had homes. Their land had been sold. Homelessness increased.

Boarding schools were not a specific part of the termination experiment, and the schools continued to receive government funding. But students everywhere were affected by what the policy meant to their own tribes and homes. A new undercurrent of worry and uncertainty ran through their daily routines. Schools changed at different paces, and some remained strict. Others, like Chilocco, took positive steps. It was during Donna's second year, in 1954, that the marching was stopped by Superintendent Correll. Without the marching on campus, Chilocco became less of a hard-core military institution. It took on a more academic feel. Some military education remained, especially for the boys. The National Guard unit still thrived.

But military training was gradually replaced by academics and athletics. In 1968, some years after Donna's time at Chilocco, the US National Guard was decommissioned at Chilocco and moved off campus.

Superintendent Correll might have helped wipe out painful punishments at Chilocco, but certain kinds of discipline lingered. Donna saw it take its toll on kids. The main tool now used to keep kids in line was a system of demerits. If students gained several demerits per week, and then more per month, they would be denied the extracurricular activities they looked forward to. Social hours were held every day after school from seven to nine p.m., between dinner and homework. But they were only for students who didn't have any demerits. The students could listen to music and talk with one another. If they had money, they could buy Cokes and chips at a concession stand. On Saturday night the socials were much larger, sometimes with live bands and dancing. They'd have snacks and play games like the Hokey Pokey. For Halloween, Christmas, and New Year's Eve, the events were even bigger. Kids with demerits missed them all. Such actions did little to make kids act "better." It simply made them more bitter.

Sometimes the students were given treats. On Sunday morning, church was mandatory for all students. But Sunday afternoon was the big treat of the week. It was movie day! The movies were sent to Chilocco just after they finished their opening theater runs. Some were recent hits. Others were classic films that had been around for a while. One often-shown movie was *Stagecoach*, from 1939. This western starred the famous actor John Wayne. It was an American classic for sure, but it certainly vilified the Indians. We were painted as "savages," often on the same level as wild animals. John Wayne and the film's director, John Ford, were known for demeaning American Indians. And, sadly, most Americans' understanding of American Indians was based on those movies.

If you had been in the audience with those Indian students watching a movie like *Stagecoach*, this is what you would have seen: Indian actors mindlessly and loudly riding toward John Wayne, with no cover. (Despite the fact that every Indian actor was a skilled horseman and trained to travel stealthily.) John Wayne would jump out from his hiding place, level his gun, and take a shot. Three or four Indians would drop dead from that *single* shot! Then the Indian students would cheer.

Even family films like those from Disney had terrible depictions of Indian characters. In the 1953 film *Peter Pan*, Wendy and the Lost Boys encounter a tribe of "red men" whose skin is bright crayon red. The children make fun of the Indians saying "How," a word that comes from the ancient and beautiful Lakota greeting *Hau*. Tiger Lily is saved from Captain Hook by Peter Pan, when her own knowledge and skill would never allow her to be captured by him in the first place.

Over the decades, things didn't improve. In 1995, the animated film *Pocahontas* was still far from true as it told the story of a young woman who falls in love with the explorer John Smith. In reality her name was Amonute, and she was eleven years old. Rather than having a romantic relationship with John Smith, her relationship was professional. She was a bright young girl who was a natural diplomat. She quickly learned English to help the colonists communicate and trade for food. Their way of paying her back was to kidnap her, force her to marry the Virginia planter John Rolfe, and send her to England. Like a carnival show, she was paraded through society as an example of how America's "savages" could be "civilized." Amonute died of pneumonia on the ship back to Virginia in 1617. She was about twenty years old. Then came Disney's *Pocahontas II* (1998), and a later film, *The New World* (2005). Both still got Pocahontas wrong.

In observance of Indigenous Peoples' Day, on October 12, in 2020, a focus group was put together by the media company React. A moderator asked American Indians of all ages to watch clips from these and other films. Their reactions were mixed. Young people said that "this is disgraceful." Older people, whose family members or who themselves had attended boarding schools, said they thought the stories were good. They had grown up with them. One said he had a crush on the animated Pocahontas. They had bought into the white man's perspective.

At last, in 2023, there was a hint of change when a new *Peter Pan* was released by Disney, this time with real Indian actors. Alyssa Wapanatâhk of the Bigstone Cree First Nation of Canada portrayed Tiger Lily. In the film she speaks the Cree language, wears authentic Cree clothing and a traditional hairstyle, and practices Cree customs. She is a smart, skilled, and courageous individual, respected by her tribe and white society. If Hollywood can finally get it right for a fictional character in a fictional book, then it's time to tell the true story of Amonute (Pocahontas), too.

These are just some examples of how well the filmmakers and actors vilified the American Indian in the twentieth century. Those cheering students watching *Stagecoach* underscored just how successful Pratt's motto, "Kill the Indian . . . and save the man," had become. We have been fighting those images and Hollywood's concept of Indians for many years, trying to set the record straight. To remain true to our history. To show that Indians were not always the bad guys.

While some students were cheering at the white-centric films, however, others were watching with resistance in their hearts. They had learned enough of the white ways to know that their own people could never fully accept that world. A different, positive change had to come. As the 1960s approached, that change was in the wind.

AMERICAN INDIANS IN HOLLYWOOD

Hollywood films on cowboys and Indians got their start in Oklahoma on the Miller Brothers 101 Ranch, not far from my Ponca family's home. In the early 1900s, the owners grew famous for their Wild West extravaganzas featuring "wild" Indians dancing in feathered regalia, hunting buffalo, and "scalping" enemies. Soon they partnered with the famous showman Buffalo Bill. The show toured the world spreading the false and degrading stereotypes of "savage" American Indians while it celebrated the "peaceful" white man's settlement of the West. The Indian actors played roles because it was a way to earn a living and feed their families.

Such shows caught the attention of big Hollywood film producers such as Thomas Ince, Cecil B. DeMille, and D. W. Griffith. Soon they were hiring the actors for the silver screen. But their false representation of Indians only grew deeper and reached even wider audiences. Roles for prominent and respected Chiefs would go to white actors, while Indian actors were cast in supporting roles. In the same roles,

Indians were paid less than non-Indian actors. In 1926, American Indian actors formed the War Paint Club, which later became the Indian Actor's Association. They demanded to be paid the same as other actors and to receive more realistic roles.

Today, American Indian actors join the nationwide Screen Actors Guild, which fights for actors' rights and equal pay. Now there are more TV shows and films telling realistic stories being made by American Indian artists. These include Zacharias Kunuk's Inuit legend *Atanarjuat: The Fast Runner* (2001) and Sterlin Harjo's documentary about his people's Muskogee-Creek hymns, *This May Be the Last Time* (2014), among many others. In 2009, Sterlin Harjo, along with my relative Migizi Pensoneau and others, formed a group called The 1491s. (That is the year before Columbus's arrival, when our land was still ours.) Out of that group, and working with Taika Waititi, came the critically acclaimed and award-winning show *Reservation Dogs* (2021-2023). In June 2022, *Dark Winds*, a cop drama series for television premiered, based on the novels of Navajo journalist Tony Hillerman. These are just a few of the TV shows and movies being made by Indian creators, starring Indian actors, telling Indian stories.

CHAPTER EIGHT

It's OK to Be an Indian!

By the end of the 1950s, American Indian boarding schools were highly successful at conditioning Indian children to be like white people. Students who had graduated boarding school and moved on to work or college tried to fit into white society. After generations of their families attending boarding schools, students' desire to follow their own culture had been replaced by a need to follow the mainstream American culture. While white American culture had been heavily borrowed from European colonizers, it was also influenced by peoples from every part of Earth. It was once called a melting pot. That is, a mixture of hundreds of cultures, melted in a single pot and stirred, so that a person does not know how to define their own family's heritage.

Our American Indian culture could never be part of a melting pot with other cultures. It is a strong, continuous lineage of people who have been on this continent for thousands of years. It is built on a single timeline in which its evolution, or development, makes sense for the peoples it represents. Fortunately, the concept of a "melting pot" has changed over time. Today, it is replaced by terms such as *mosaic*. Just as many different glass pieces make a whole mosaic, so do many people from distinctive cultures make an entire society. Each piece or person influences the others but keeps a singular identity.

Until the 1960s, American Indian students did not question or speak out against the way the boarding schools compelled their culture to dissolve into the big American melting pot. But a cowering, beat-down dog can only take so much. If you keep striking it with a stick, at some point it will strike back. Many found individual ways to hold on to the most precious parts of their culture. They might share their own unique tribal traditions among themselves, sometimes in secret. Dance, slang, and stories are just a few cultural items they exchanged. While the practices might differ slightly from tribe to tribe, the basic traditions were shared between all tribes. They were familiar to all students. They gave students comfort and connection to their ancient heritage. As American Indian high school students borrowed from one another, they began to have a new understanding of and respect for their culture.

This sharing would lead to a nationwide renewal of American Indian identity and culture. For some tribal individuals, this meant reinforcing the Native culture they knew. For others, it meant rebuilding their culture from scratch. From the early 1960s through the 1970s, college and university students began looking more closely in the mirror. They saw an American

Chilocco School parade float, with students in Native dress.

Indian because of their features and the color of their skin. But they were dressed like a white person. They talked like a white person. They had to ask themselves, *What kind of Indian am I?* This was not only happening at the college and university level. High school students were asking that question as well. Richard Henry Pratt's policy, "Kill the Indian . . . and save the man," had influenced generations. But had Pratt truly succeeded? Had American Indian culture truly been erased?

From out of the wilderness came a firm and well-spoken voice. "We are not free. We do not make choices. Our choices are made for us." These words came from one of our own people. Clyde

Warrior was a Ponca tribal member and himself a college student at Cameron Junior College and later at Northeastern State, both in Oklahoma. Clyde had recently founded the National Indian Youth Council (NIYC) and been elected its first president.

Clyde Warrior was raised by his grandmother, instilling in him all the knowledge of his Ponca culture. He spoke our Ponca language. He was a singer at the sacred drum, which reinforces spiritual connection to our heritage. He was also a champion Fancy Dancer, a form of dance based on the war dance and created by the Ponca tribe in the early 1900s to preserve our culture. His grandmother was a strong woman, who believed deeply in protecting Ponca culture because she was a survivor of Chilocco. She was Metha Gives Water Collins, the girl who had the coins ripped from her hair. Clyde would become the lightning bolt for his grandmother's justice and for the justice of American Indians across the nation.

Clyde was a natural leader. He was passionate and articulate. Metha also made sure Clyde was well educated at the white man's colleges so he knew their ways. All of this made him well equipped to pull his people up from the cultural genocide they'd experienced. And he did.

My first memories of Clyde changed my life. I remember a gathering at my grandmother Elizabeth's home in Ponca City when I was nine years old. The kids played outside as her home slowly filled with Ponca Elders. Many of the women wore Indian dresses.

Clyde Warrior.

The Elder men wore black shirts and big white cowboy hats. The women were bringing various foods into Grandma's kitchen, and we young boys were hovering around the screen doors and poking our heads through the open windows, trying to figure out a way to get in and raid the frybread baskets. The cook's assistants kept a close eye on us. If they caught us coming too close, they would swat at us with towels they draped around their shoulders. They used those towels to keep the kitchen clean as they worked. Some towels were half wet and made formidable whips.

Then Clyde came. He was the last to arrive, and we watched him, a younger man, walk into the middle of a house full of Elders. You would have had to see Clyde to really know the impact he made. There was a confidence he carried, the way he dressed, and even the way he walked. He began speaking to the Elders, sometimes in Ponca, sometimes in English. He wasn't an Elder, but the way he commanded the floor and the way he spoke, and their reaction to him, told us they had a deep respect for him. His entrance that day showed me, more than anything else ever had, that you can be a special person in your Elders' eyes and with your people. It influenced my life seeing Clyde on that one day. I had seen him at other times, but not like this.

While Clyde was working toward his college bachelor's degree in those days, he learned all he could about being a successful voice for his people. During this time, the civil rights movement, led by the renowned reverend Dr. Martin Luther King Jr. was gaining world attention. Clyde actively reached out and worked with prominent members of the movement. He found a mentor in the famous comedian and activist Dick Gregory. He sought out Dr. King himself and learned his ways of speaking out for African American justice with strong but peaceful words, and even walked hand in hand with him during a nonviolent march against the Vietnam War held in New York City in 1967. Clyde spoke out and held workshops through his own organization, the National Indian Youth Council. He used all the tools he had learned to help his people recover their pride and heritage. Soon he began to make a name for himself.

Protestors during the April 15, 1967, march against the Vietnam War in New York City.

Clyde worked hard to repeal the Termination Policy, crossing the nation to speak out against it. He also spoke against incompetent leadership in the Bureau of Indian Affairs, which had been relocating his people. He helped tribes in Washington State to secure fishing rights that had been taken from them. He met with Native community leaders to discuss solutions for extreme poverty. He pushed people to organize and advocate for themselves.

In the mid-1960s, Clyde wrote two famous essays: "Which One Are You? Five Types of Young Indians" and "We Are Not Free." The essays spoke out against poverty, discrimination, and

Native American youths protest to demand the return of land from the Fort Lawton army base in Seattle.

oppression of American Indian Nations. They called for pride in Native heritage with its origins in the continent over thousands of years ago. He wrote, "The sewage of Europe does not run through these veins."

Many news outlets reported that Clyde was taking a radical approach to bring about change in the living conditions of American Indians. They said that Clyde was following the teachings of the radical Black movements. He had coined the phrase *Red Power*, mirroring the term *Black Power*. But Clyde was no radical. In fact, nothing could be further from the truth. Clyde was following his own family's cultural and tribal legacy. That includes the legacy of Standing Bear. To all in our Ponca tribe, Standing Bear is our ancestral great-grandfather. Not every Ponca member is blood-related to him, but we all have a tribal relationship based on respect. Chief Standing Bear was a strong and peaceful leader whom we all wish to emulate.

Now, nearly a hundred years after Standing Bear's victory, Clyde was following in his ancestor's footsteps. He was speaking out for justice. He spoke across college campuses. He became an editor for the national newspaper *Indian Voices*. News stations sought him out for television interviews. In an interview with NBC, Clyde spoke about who American Indians really are. He listed several categories that young American Indians could use to define their own selfhood and life experiences. He was slowly waking up the Indian in all American Indians, far and wide, throughout Indian Country. "It's OK to be an Indian!" he told the people. When Clyde's message came out, it spread through Indian Country like a prairie fire.

If you were an American Indian, that simple statement had deep meaning. After one hundred years of trying to be something they were not, American Indians were hearing this young, smart, handsome, and articulate American Indian man tell them they didn't have to strive to be white. In those six short words, *It's OK to be an Indian*, Clyde was handing the children and young adults of the Indian Nations a magic key that would unlock their identity. As American Indians, they could look to the future with hope and possibility and pride. We had suffered so much internal conflict, knowing we were Indian but being forced to act "white." Such conflict had haunted my generation and that of my parents and grandparents. Now that conflict could end.

We didn't have to stop being an Indian to get a good education. We didn't have to be a white person to live our lives. *It's OK to be an Indian!* While Clyde's message was designed for older students, high school students had their ear to the ground as well. They shared the same identity problems as their older brothers and sisters. Clyde's message was just as profound to that group of young people.

Clyde became a national hero. His words ignited the hopes and dreams of American Indian youth from all tribes. But to

STANDING BEAR'S VICTORY

When the US Army, under General George Crook, forced Standing Bear's Ponca tribe from their ancestral homeland in Nebraska to Oklahoma in 1877, the people suffered and many died, including Standing Bear's sixteen-year-old son, Bear Shield. Crook and his army did not care that these people should have rights under the United States Constitution. Indians were not considered "persons" under the law. Bear Shield's final wish was to be buried in his homeland, not in a foreign place where his spirit would wander. Determined to honor him, Standing Bear carried his son's remains and led a small group of mourners back to their ancestral grounds. The army soon arrested them as a "renegade" band that had deserted their tribe.

A local newspaperman and two lawyers came to Standing Bear's defense. The lawyers presented the case *Chief Standing Bear v. General George Crook* before the Nebraska court. They argued that Standing Bear and his clan were, indeed, "persons" under the law and had the right to move where they pleased, just like anyone else. The judge and courtroom seemed to see this as just another case in which Indians resisted being moved. The court would no doubt rule against it. Then, in the final moments, Standing Bear stood up. The shocked courtroom fell silent. An Indian would not have the right to speak! But the judge nodded.

Standing Bear extended his right hand and held it still for several moments. Then he spoke. "That hand," he said, "is not the color of yours, but if I pierce it, I shall feel pain. If you pierce your hand, you also feel pain. The blood that will flow from mine will be of the same color as yours. I am a man. The same God made us both." Next he told a simple story of the desperation his people faced. "We are weak and faint and sick," he said, adding, "One man bars our passage" to a safer place. He turned to the judge. "You are that man." Quietly, Standing Bear sat down. He had made his case. He had held that Indians be treated equally under the Constitution, as human beings and American citizens. He was the first American Indian ever to bring a civil rights case against the United States of America. And he was also the first to win one.

our Ponca community, he was simply Clyde, Metha's grandson. There is a saying, "You can never be a hero in your own hometown." I think that line was written for Clyde. He was working on a national level. But we at the reservation didn't really understand this. For the most part we didn't really care. Life on our reservation was hard. Everybody had their own problems to deal with. That pretty much took priority over everything else. But whenever Clyde could visit, we welcomed him home. And he fit right in.

The Ponca have a strong belief that "not one of us is any better than any other of us. What is good for one of us is good for all of us." We learn this from an early age. That belief seems at odds with practices in the greater white society. That is, it conflicts with people's need to "climb the ladder" above others in business, to make more money than others, or to achieve fame. At some points it seems to conflict with my own American Indian society. But here is the difference: If members of our tribe are rewarded with better jobs and more income than the others, they are expected to do more for those who can't fend for themselves. Clyde was one of those members.

For several years I was just too young to fully realize the impact Clyde was making across Indian Country and within our own Ponca Nation. I didn't read his essays until I was at college myself. Then I began to understand who he was. He worked on a national level. He was not a spokesperson for the

RED POWER IS BORN
Remembering with Della Warrior

Clyde Warrior coined the term *Red Power* during a parade. Years later, his widow, Della Warrior, recalled that day. The annual convention for the National Congress of American Indians (NCAI) was being held in Oklahoma City. Clyde and his group of friends and supporters were going to participate in the parade.

"Clyde, Mel Thom, Bruce Wilkie, Hank Adams, and I were getting ready for it," said Della. "They rented a convertible, and I was the driver." The group wanted to put signs on the convertible that instilled pride in being Indian and were trying to decide what slogans to write on them. "At the time," Della explained, "Clyde was being called a communist." Communism was a big concern across the United States in the 1950s and 1960s. US leaders held that the Soviet Union's communist beliefs endangered democracy. The two nations refused to cooperate and held a standoff called the Cold War. Both had powerful weapons, and if either nation overstepped its bounds, the other might launch the weapons to start a real war. Clyde was standing up and stating that American Indians and all other ethnicities should have the same rights as white society. He was calling for the return of land for the people to share.

Soon he was labeled a "radical and a communist" in an editorial in the *Tulsa World* newspaper and by other groups. Clyde knew that communism was represented by the color red. In addition, the Black Power Movement was already underway and was getting a lot of publicity for the slogan *Black Power.* So, Clyde and the group put it all together. "They jokingly said, 'Let's call ourselves Red Power,'" said Della. "They laughed and wrote *Red Power* on the signs." Soon the term represented a new era of revitalizing American Indian culture.

Ponca or any one tribe. He had gone intertribal, meaning he was a spokesman for all tribes. His work raised the national awareness of the American Indian people, and it opened doors for all Indian Nations. I learned that this is how he gave back.

According to our Ponca ethic, everyone is treated the same. Clyde indeed stood up for everyone. At the same time most

Ponca are fearless individuals. Again, that was Clyde. Fearless. Unique. He traveled tirelessly from coast to coast spreading his message. Today, Clyde's very large family rightly holds Clyde's legacy in the highest esteem. And there are many other families in the tribe that also regard Clyde with the deepest respect. He brought honor to his tribe and to all American Indians.

Because of Clyde's tireless activism, working with American Indian leaders like Ada Deer and with the committed young followers she inspired, the US government began taking a new look at long-standing laws and broken treaties. In 1968, the Johnson administration called for the repeal of the Termination Policy of 1953. "Fortunately, through a national battle, we still have our treaty rights," said Della Warrior. "Imagine the Indian World if the policy intent had been carried out. The government would no longer be obligated to provide services to us. We would not have dual citizenship and would be regular citizens. What little land tribes and individuals have would probably have been sold for our inability to pay taxes on it."

Although exposure of abuse and brainwashing in American Indian boarding schools had begun with the Meriam Report in 1928, many schools had returned to "business as usual" for the next thirty years. Now again the ongoing abuse and brainwashing were being exposed. Better and more far-reaching media—newspapers, radio, and television—spread the word. One by one, the schools closed.

Like a shooting star, Clyde's career shone brightly but briefly. Near the end of the 1960s, he was diagnosed with liver disease from living a high-stress life, which included drinking alcohol. He was only twenty-eight years old. Just before he died, in 1968, he heard President Lyndon Johnson's speech "The Forgotten American," proposing the end of the Termination Policy. Clyde Warrior could die in peace. His words continued to ring across the nation, in the ears of every American Indian. To be an American Indian was to have "Red Power"—and to be proud of it.

CHAPTER NINE

Red Power Continues

In 1969, a government finding called the Kennedy Report laid bare the US government's hand in nearly a hundred years of neglect and abuse in American Indian education. "A major indictment of our failure," the report said. The world was stunned. Why had no one known?

Formally titled *Indian Education: A National Tragedy—A National Challenge*, the report was authored by Senators Edward and Robert F. Kennedy, both major civil rights supporters. After a year spent investigating Indian school systems and the assassination of Robert, Edward and a committee in Congress listed outrageous statistics. Some school dropout rates approached 100 percent, and achievement levels were two to three years below that of white students. Indian children believed themselves to be "below average" in intelligence. "Our failure to provide an effective education for the American Indian has condemned him to a life of poverty and despair," the committee wrote.

The report provided a plan for reworking the entire school system and for reinstating pride in heritage. Indian culture would be taught in all classrooms. Parents would be involved in forming school policy. Tribal communities would operate their own schools. Most important, the Bureau of Indian Affairs would be reorganized because its white officials had been careless and uncaring, working against change and innovation. The Kennedy Report raised awareness of the plight of Indian students and families everywhere. It denounced a century of horrors of the boarding school era started by Richard Henry Pratt and the United States Congress with the expressed aim of wiping out Indigenous culture. It presented a hopeful and workable plan. And change began.

But the wheels of government continued to churn slowly. In 1972, the Indian Education Act established the Office of Indian Education and the National Advisory Council on Indian Education. The government provided federal funds to empower American Indians to manage their own education system. In 1975, the Self-Determination and Education Assistance Act gave tribes the right to administer their own federal programs, which included government boarding schools. Some boarding schools remained, and some with unthinkable practices. It took until 1978 for an important piece of legislation, the Indian Child Welfare Act, to be passed by Congress. At last, parents' cries had reached the lawmakers' ears—do not take our children away! The ICWA gave parents the right to refuse sending their children to off-reservation schools. Enrollments petered out. At last, my family's own school, Chilocco, closed its doors in 1980. Still,

America had a long way to go to make changes to American Indian education and to bury the legacy of pain and cultural destruction the schools had caused. There were yet *more* miles to travel to restore American Indian lands and rights.

Some American Indians could not wait for the government to take the lead. They stepped in to carry on Clyde Warrior's legacy. That legacy had made immediate impacts in the 1960s and 1970s. Clyde's words and actions inspired the founders of a new, high-profile activist organization who called themselves the American Indian Movement (AIM). The year Clyde died, in 1968, two American Indians, Dennis Banks and Clyde Bellecourt, were serving time in a Minnesota prison when they came together to establish AIM. They had both been convicted of robbing grocery stores to feed their families. Soon they were joined by others, including Clyde's brother, Vernon Bellecourt, and a civil rights activist named Russell Means.

Through AIM, the group carried on the work they admired in Clyde Warrior. Like Clyde, they fought for Native American civil rights and antiracism. Their work began in Minneapolis and spread to other big cities, where they spoke out against poverty and police brutality. Soon they widened the issues to unemployment, poor education, Indians' stolen lands, and the lack of support for cultural practices. At times they took Clyde's term of *Red Power* to an extreme. Sometimes their actions turned dark.

In 1969, AIM leaders gathered hundreds of protestors and

Russell Means (left) and Dennis Banks (right).

occupied the prison on Alcatraz Island, in the San Francisco Bay. For a year and a half, they refused to leave. They called for answers to their requests for better education, better housing, better health care, and fair treatment by the police. At last, they were evacuated by the US government in 1971. But their demands had not been met. So, in 1972, AIM and other groups, including Clyde Warrior's own National Indian Youth Council as well as the Survival of American Indians Association, marched from Seattle and Los Angeles to Washington, DC. Their walk was known as the Trail of Broken Treaties. With them, leaders carried a document called "The Twenty Points Position Paper." It held twenty demands to the US government to restore some 110 million acres of American Indian lands, to institute civil rights, and to improve government

Unidentified Trail of Broken Treaties protestor in Washington, DC.

relations. The AIM members were especially concerned by useless and underhanded actions they had witnessed within the Bureau of Indian Affairs (BIA). They wanted the bureau replaced with a new Office of Indian Relations.

AIM AT ALCATRAZ ISLAND

In 1934, Alcatraz was a United States maximum-security prison for dangerous criminals such as Al "Scarface" Capone and George "Machine Gun" Kelly. A remote island in the waters off the coast of San Francisco, California, it was thought to be an excellent place for prisoners because escape was impossible. But after a few decades, the prison got so expensive to run that the government closed it.

The American Indian Movement, newly formed in 1968, saw an opportunity. They claimed that the land should be theirs, citing an 1868 treaty that said Indians could take over any unused federal lands. They asked the US government to turn the old prison into an Indian cultural center, museum, and school. But the government, under President Richard Nixon, refused. AIM would not give up. They set their plans in motion.

In 1969, a group called Indians of All Tribes sailed across San Francisco Bay and occupied the old prison. They wrote a letter to President Nixon, addressing it to "The Great White Father and All His People." In it, they claimed the land for American Indians. President Nixon sent negotiators to talk them out of it. The negotiators stressed that the island had no electricity or running water. They could have other land in California. *We're used to this environment*, replied the new occupants. *It's no different from living on our poverty-stricken reservations.* The people especially looked up to a charismatic young leader, Richard Oakes, whom they called the mayor of Alcatraz. They elected a council and worked together to set up housing, sanitation, schools, day care, and a large kitchen for shared meals. Supporters on the mainland paid for electricity and sent water barrels on barges.

For the next year, Alcatraz hummed with life. Still, the government and AIM could not see eye to eye. Because there was no resolution, people grew tired of waiting and the community began to fall apart. Oakes and the other leaders quarreled. Some people left to find jobs on the mainland. College students went back to school. Oakes left after his stepdaughter died in a terrible accident falling down an old stairwell.

Eventually, the government turned off the electricity and blocked the water deliveries. In the final months of 1970, the remaining people were hungry and cold. Fights broke out. There were murders. On June 10, 1971, the FBI and US special forces swarmed the island and removed the final few occupants.

Many thought the Alcatraz occupation had failed. But far more people knew it had been a success. AIM had raised awareness about the unfair treaties, the poverty, and the lack of resources suffered by all Indian Nations. As a result, President Nixon officially ended the 1953 Termination Policy. Now, Native families would govern their own communities and preserve their own heritage. Thousands of acres of ancestral land were immediately returned, with millions more to come. This support gave confidence to the American Indian Movement and other Native activists. Today their descendants continue fighting for the rights of all Indian Nations. That includes ensuring that government and religious groups make reparations to families who suffered in boarding schools.

Occupation of Alcatraz protestors.

Before leaving the West Coast, the AIM leaders had scheduled meetings with President Nixon and members of Congress. In addition, the BIA had promised to reserve special housing for the group. But once they arrived in Washington, DC, the AIM marchers learned that the meetings had been canceled. The housing had never been reserved. The once-peaceful demonstrators were angry and frustrated. They mobbed the Department of the Interior, which houses the Bureau of Indian Affairs. Once inside, the demonstrators barricaded the doors against police. In anger, they overturned desks, ripped open file cabinets, and spray-painted walls. Then they established a camp and set about doing important work.

For the next week they scoured documents in hundreds of boxes of BIA records. They found reams of papers revealing BIA mismanagement of lands and theft of funds and resources reserved for American Indians. This made their cries even louder. To calm the demonstrators, the Nixon administration formed a task force to address the BIA wrongdoings and to discuss the list of Twenty Points with AIM leaders. At last, after a week, the demonstrators agreed to leave. The BIA offices had been extensively damaged, but the Nixon administration dropped all charges and paid the way home for the demonstrators. Once the people had left, however, the new task force did little to address their demands. Fortunately, future administrations did. Gradually, congressional champions for the Twenty

Protestors occupying the Bureau of Indian Affairs.

Points helped turn them into concrete American Indian policy. The reversal of past policies gained steam into the twenty-first century. AIM's actions had catalyzed change. Dennis Banks wrote, "We had sent up one hell of a smoke signal."

A year later, in 1973, the smoke signal burst into flames. Sioux leaders in South Dakota called AIM to help them at the Pine Ridge Reservation. This was the birthplace of Russell Means, so he was soon on the way, joined by Dennis Banks. They discovered that the reservation's Sioux leaders were rebelling against the tribal chairman, Richard Wilson, because they believed he was a corrupt puppet of the BIA and did not stand up for his people. The tribe had separated into two factions and had taken up arms against each other. Local white lawmakers had been called in. Then came the FBI.

The world watched what would happen next. Most people knew Pine Ridge as the infamous site of the Wounded Knee Massacre in 1890. In a bloody massacre, the US Cavalry killed between 150 and 300 innocent Sioux who were practicing their tribal Ghost Dance. Now, almost eighty years later, it looked as if tragedy would strike again. Residents of the reservation, tribal police, government agents, US marshals, and the FBI took sides. Celebrities,

Federal troops blocking the road to Wounded Knee during the 1973 standoff.

WOUNDED KNEE MASSACRE, 1890

The Lakota Sioux had once freely hunted buffalo on the plains. By the 1880s, they had been forced onto reservations, to grow crops, wear western dress, and send their children away to boarding schools. Food was scarce. The people were starving and desperate. They were ready to listen to a prophet named Wovoka.

Wovoka practiced a long-standing ceremony called the Ghost Dance. One night, after a powerful dream, he told the people that if they remained peaceful and practiced the Ghost Dance, God would help them. He would bury the white people deep under the ground. Earth would return to its natural state, and the Indian Nations would be free. The Ghost Dance movement spread.

US administrators at the Lakota reservation grew frightened. They called in the US Army to stop the movement. But one horrible incident led to another. First, the powerful leader Sitting Bull refused to let the army stop the dancers. Sitting Bull's Lakota Sioux had joined Crazy Horse's Cheyenne in the Battle of Little Bighorn in 1876. Now, Sitting Bull and his people lived peacefully, but he would not let the army take away his people's dance. The army tried to arrest Sitting Bull. When people tried to protect their Chief, the army fired, killing Sitting Bull and other Lakotas. The soldiers continued to Wounded Knee Creek to stop another band of Ghost Dancers.

When they arrived, they ordered the dancers to surrender their few weapons. But one dancer was deaf and did not understand what was happening. He refused to give up his rifle and fighting broke out. A shot was fired. Immediately, the US soldiers fired on the group of dancers. It was a brutal massacre. In the end, more than 150 Indian people lay dead, mostly women and children. In a terrible lie, the Bureau of Indian Affairs reported the massacre as a fair fight. The soldiers received Congressional Medals of Honor. The Lakota dead were buried in a mass grave in the middle of winter.

philanthropists, and religious leaders came to support one faction or the other. Russell Means, Dennis Banks, and the AIM members again demanded an investigation of the inept Bureau of Indian Affairs.

AIM held eleven Sioux as hostages until they could get the answer they wanted. But the government agents wouldn't budge. The standoff continued for seventy-one days. During that time, federal agents gunned down two Sioux. Over the weeks, many people from both factions were wounded. At last, government officials promised to investigate AIM's complaints. AIM surrendered, and Russell Means and Dennis Banks were arrested. Soon, however, the charges were dropped against them. It seems the US government had unlawfully handled both the witnesses and the evidence in the affair.

The AIM organization had no direct effect on my family, and I wasn't a member or supporter of it, but I will never forget their occupation of the Wounded Knee burial site near the Pine Ridge Reservation. It was a very good thing and a long overdue statement by American Indians about our treatment by the United States. I had many relatives who were involved there in leadership positions. My uncle Carter Camp was in charge of AIM's security at the time, and I was proud of him for that. He really put his life on the line for what he believed in.

I was a Tribal Council member in 2001, when one of AIM's leaders later received national attention and lots of press for all the wrong reasons. Russell Means had physically abused his Navajo wife and her father, a military veteran who had lost an arm during World War II. The Navajo Nation put out a warrant for his arrest, but Russell Means turned against the Indian system he had worked so hard to support. In an unusual betrayal of his own people, he appealed to a US federal court. He said that the Navajo Nation did not have the sovereign authority to bring him back to the reservation for a trial. The non-Indian court was eager to agree with Russell. While the white government saved Russell from having to face his crimes, he was setting a horrible precedent for all the tribes in America. Each Native government must be allowed to pursue the people who commit crimes on our lands, even if they run off the reservation to escape justice. As far as I'm concerned, the legacy Russell Means left for Indian justice is one of hypocrisy. But he was just one of AIM's leaders. The others have only fought for American Indian rights with honor.

Despite its dark periods, AIM had been heard. In the true spirit of Clyde Warrior, the group inspired cultural renewal across the nation. Over time, its members have been teachers and speakers who guide adults and children to learn and appreciate their languages and heritage. They have established employment programs in cities and in rural reservation communities. Well into the twenty-first century, AIM has remained a catalyst for reinstating American Indian rights. They have reintroduced traditions and demanded respect for American Indian lands and practices.

In 1991, Clyde Bellecourt and other AIM members helped restore the Sun Dance, a ceremony of dancing, prayer, and renewal, that had been forbidden by the US government since 1904. The first revival ceremony was held at Minnesota's Pipestone National Monument, a land sacred to our people. In the early 2000s, Clyde's brother, Vernon, helped lead the fight to change the names of national football and other athletic teams, like the Washington Redskins (now the Washington Commanders), and to ban mascots wearing Indian costumes during games.

Soon AIM's global impact became clear. AIM's actions at Wounded Knee had opened the door for other American Indian tribes to take their cases to court. To win back their rightful lands. To practice their traditions. To keep their families together. To reinstate tribal laws and courts. Those actions inspired Indigenous communities around the world to claim their rights, too. The movement's finest global hour came in 2007, when the United Nations passed the international Declaration on the Rights of Indigenous Peoples. The declaration honored the cultural and ceremonial expression, identity, language, employment, health, and education of all Indigenous peoples. It was a day of celebration for the global Indigenous communities whom AIM had helped unite.

At home, AIM had increased awareness of major changes needed in the Bureau of Indian Affairs. In 1977, the position of assistant secretary of Indian Affairs was established. Since then, all its appointees have been American Indians. In addition, the BIA has increased the number of American Indian and Alaska Natives working in the Bureau so that, as of 2024, most of its employees are Indigenous, with a focus on the needs of their people. The work to ensure that every community can realize the vision of Clyde Warrior and of AIM continues. That every American Indian child can be proud to be an Indian. That every child will use their Red Power for good.

FOR FUTURE GENERATIONS

In 2007, Clyde Warrior's legacy became a permanent symbol of our Ponca tribe and of all American Indian perseverance. A circular structure that mirrors our traditional tribal roundhouses, the Clyde Warrior Memorial opened in White Eagle, the headquarters for the Ponca Tribe of Indians of Oklahoma. While designed to reflect our ancient heritage on the outside, its interior is very modern. That combination of new and old truly says *Clyde Warrior*. It also reflects the American Indian's unique ability to live in two worlds, of ancient heritage and the ever-changing present.

When the building was at last dedicated in 2018, a time capsule containing precious Ponca items was buried beside it. Clyde Warrior would have applauded this time capsule designed by the Ponca Tribe of Indians of Oklahoma with the Smithsonian National Museum of the American Indian. Made of stainless steel, it is eight feet long and six feet wide and carefully sealed so that the historic items inside will remain safe for 130 years (the length of time our people have lived in Oklahoma), until 2148. Its engineers hold that it is strong enough even to last underwater for 500 years. More than 2,000 Ponca songs and stories, dried foods, photographs, tools, clothing, our history and beliefs, a large ceremonial drum, full dance regalia, maps of our traditional tribal lands, our tribal rules, and more, will one day greet our future people, providing them a link to the past and inspiring them to move forward with pride.

CHAPTER TEN

Chilocco Closes

Chilocco had gone through changes in its hundred-year history, from being built by Italian immigrant and American Indian student laborers in the 1800s, to being showcased in the 1920s as a model agricultural mecca. It was well on its way in 1904 when an article appeared in the *Cherokee Messenger* that stated, "The *Indian School Journal* claims that Chilocco is the only real agricultural college for Indians in the country." There was nothing like it in the world, touted a 1923 issue of Chilocco's *Indian School Journal* after the school had been praised in a national agricultural magazine. Chilocco worked with the Oklahoma State University Agricultural Department to make improvements that have impacted American agriculture today. The soil erosion program and the breeding of Morgan horses are two enduring examples. In addition, students enjoyed a "plot" program in which they grew their own crops and sold them in farmers' markets, keeping the proceeds. The second to last superintendent was Jim Baker, a member of the Choctaw tribe and also my brother-in-law. He had met my sister Charmain

Jim Baker.

at Chilocco, and they later married. A Chilocco student from 1958 to 1960, Baker praised the school's programs. "I always tell people that Chilocco was ahead of its time, with 20 something vocational and agricultural programs on campus."

Tragically, in the early 1970s, there was a brutal murder at Chilocco, in which one student was accused of killing another student. Both were members of the Ponca tribe. It was less a reflection of the school itself and more related to the horrible conditions of displacement and poverty our people had suffered for a century. Negative press followed the incident. There were also untrue accusations by militant civil rights groups that children were being abused at Chilocco. The National Indian

Youth Council, which had become more militant after Clyde Warrior's death, sent a letter to parents that warned them of "unreasonable restraints" being put on their children. The letter said children were experiencing illegal detention, invasion of privacy, and poor recreational and counseling facilities. The group even staged a sit-in protest at the school.

An investigation was conducted by the Department of the Interior and found nothing. The Chilocco student council itself responded with a letter in the *Daily Oklahoman*, denying the claims and confirming their support for the school. Even though there was no evidence of wrongdoing at the school, the accusations were enough to damage Chilocco's reputation. Its enrollment dropped rapidly. At its highest point, it had housed some 1,400 students. Soon only 100 attended the massive school. As Ponca tribal members and oppressed people, we had learned the tools and weapons of persecution so well that we used them on one another.

Following those incidents, Chilocco once again changed. It became a school that would take on American Indian children from hardship families, orphans who had no family at all, and children who were having a hard time in public schools. In 1979, that was the situation my brother Mike's daughter Denise found herself in. She had become pregnant early in high school. Now, with a little boy to raise, she was living in the small Oklahoma town of Newkirk, which was less than open-minded. Racism was very much alive and well there. So that fall, Mike loaded her up and took her to Chilocco. There she would be a day student. She lived so close to the school that she could attend classes there and go home at night and on the weekends to be with her son. No one knew it would be the school's last year.

Denise's move to Chilocco turned out to be the best thing to happen to her. She was greeted by people who looked like her, and not just a few. It was the whole school. All of her teachers were American Indian. Thanks to AIM and other activist organizations of the 1960s and 1970s, the Bureau of Indian Affairs had received the message: Indian educators needed to resemble the students they were to educate.

Denise Jones.

When Denise left Newkirk to enter Chilocco in her junior year of high school, she had fallen behind in her studies. Her family had previously lived in Dallas, where Mike was a master printer. There Denise had attended strong schools through the sixth grade. When Mike moved the family back to Oklahoma, he enrolled Denise in the Newkirk public school. The education standards of white Oklahoma schools were low at the time. "I was bored," she said. "There wasn't anything to do, except a little mischief. I found that pretty good!" It didn't help that she was Indian. She never received the mentoring that would have enabled her to shine in her classes. Denise said she had not learned to write a story or compose a research paper. By the time she was a sophomore in high school, she was reading at a level far beneath her grade and age. When she entered Chilocco as a junior, Denise was immediately assigned a special counselor named Sandra Fife to help bring her reading and writing up to their standards. Unlike the public school, Chilocco's standards were competitive on a national level.

If not criminal, then it was a crying shame what Oklahoma lawmakers had done to the state's educational system. Instead of properly funding the schools to keep up with the national standards, records show that lawmakers poured state funds and resources into oil and gas companies where they were shareholders. The lawmakers simply wanted more profits. Their children and those of other wealthy families could go to private schools. But the rest of the children across the state suffered.

During Denise's time at Chilocco, she continued living with her family in nearby Newkirk. When she went into the town, she was often referred to as a *squaw*, a derogatory and racist term. It was very hurtful, and she did not like to spend time there. It was just one of many towns that were unwelcoming to American Indians. Denise once said that her worst memories from Chilocco were when their teams played "away" games at the white public schools in low-income areas. She was a cheerleader and remembered that the white home team would call out racial slurs when the Indian team came out on the court or field. I've seen that racist behavior throughout my life.

THE COLD, HARD FACTS OF RACISM

When Denise stepped into the Newkirk, Oklahoma, public school, she experienced name-calling by students. Teachers and counselors displayed a lack of interest in helping her achieve academic success and plot out her future. During the 1970s, American Indian students may have been echoing Clyde Warrior's motto "It's OK to be an Indian." They may have been renewing the practice of their Indian traditions while stepping into the white world. But the white world did not necessarily agree with, or even know about, Clyde's outlook. Accepting American Indians as equals was not a priority. After more than a century of treating Indians as second-class citizens, society found it an all too easy path to continue on. Stories told by Denise and other students during the 1970s and 1980s are thick with the injustices they experienced in the white community.

Around 1980, government researchers for the first time began taking a hard look at those injustices and recording them in numbers. It went far beyond name-calling. The data showed massive inequality in education and teachers, in job opportunities and quality of jobs, in housing, in healthy environments, in education, and in access to quality health care, or to health care at all. In the early 2020s, attorneys for the Department of the Treasury began creating a series of reports based on the statistics. They showed in cold, hard terms how American Indians as well as Black and Hispanic populations had been greatly damaged over generations by a public that had not only ignored them but worked against them. And, in damaging those groups, the nation had stunted its own economic growth. It is sad that a nation sits up and takes notice only because it has missed a financial opportunity. This statistical blow, however, was joined by a deeper humanitarian crisis: the discovery in 2021 of children's unmarked graves in Canadian residential schools and in many boarding schools across the United States. The extreme cruelty dealt to American Indian populations could no longer be ignored.

Denise not only rose above such treatment, she excelled. Throughout her junior year, she was drawn to anything to do with business. She loved typing. She took math and learned marketing. She threw herself into the social whirl. She became the captain of the cheerleading squad and grew close to the teacher who coached them. She smiles when she recalls that time. "We felt like we were hot stuff!" Girls had to be true athletes to make the squad, and they were proud to cheer on the other women athletes. "Our basketball girls were tough," she said. "They were awesome!" Denise's grandmother, my mother, would have been proud of Denise's academic and athletic successes.

Besides cheerleading, Denise cultivated friendships with young people from many tribes. "Probably one of the most

Chilocco cheerleading squad in 1971.

memorable things," she said, "was my dad would always want me to bring kids home with me. He knew many were far away from their families, and some didn't have any family. They came from all different situations. Every week, I would bring one of my friends home with me."

As graduation approached for the senior class in the spring of 1980, Denise still had one year to go. She and her classmates watched the seniors take their class trip to Washington, DC, and they all looked forward to their own future trip in 1981. On graduation day, Denise and the other students sat in the audience, cheering on the graduates. Then the superintendent stepped up to the podium. Chilocco was closing, he told them. The class of 1980 had been the final class.

The undergraduates were stunned. In her one year at Chilocco, Denise had found her place and her people. Her grades had improved. She had made friends she still has today. She is a member of the Chilocco alumni and attends their annual events with hundreds of other former Chiloccoans. They love it to this day, nearly fifty years after it closed. Denise first attended those events with her father, Mike, and he never missed one. "They know how to have fun," Denise said. "There are judges and lawyers, and it's amazing to me the quality of people that Chilocco did raise. Many entrepreneurs. They were taught how to live in [white] society and succeed."

Denise herself went on to succeed as an entrepreneur. She spent her last year of high school in the white public high school Chapparal, in Kansas. She recalls it was "traumatic." But that one year at Chilocco had been a turning point. It had made her strong and self-confident. She had built the educational and social foundation to thrive. In her coming years at college and university, Denise would study broadcasting and business, then use her skills to become a radio station broadcaster and manager. She managed stores. She developed marketing plans for her family's mechanical engineering business and a medical records business. Not to mention that she raised seven children, a business in itself!

While at Oklahoma State University, Denise and her friends founded the school's Native American Student Association, and they held the school's first powwow. My sister Donna helped her put it together. Two members of my family were carrying on our tradition. In 2017, Denise was interviewed by Julie Pearson Little-Thunder for the Chilocco History Project. "What would you like people to know or remember about Chilocco?" asked Julie. Denise replied, "It was family."

Denise had experienced personal success at Chilocco. The school's closing reflected the less-than-supportive attitudes toward American Indians in the 1980s. Chilocco had opened in 1884 for the sole purpose of bringing Indians into the white world, but since the 1930s, the school had successfully integrated American Indian culture and heritage into white education. Chilocco had become an example for other boarding schools. Here, Indians could celebrate their culture while learning to live in the white world. We had finally made Chilocco a school of our own. On June 3, 1980, the federal government took that away. It was a matter of funding, they said.

The Bureau of Indian Affairs looked at Chilocco's budget and enrollment. The campus had 125 buildings, which needed electricity, water, and maintenance. The grounds needed mowing and continuous upkeep. By 1980, the student population was barely 400. It simply cost too much to keep the massive campus open for the benefit of so few people. The BIA deemed that the school was no longer worth the expense. The same was decided for Fort Sill, Seneca, and Concho Indian Schools in Oklahoma, and for others across the country. Here is the message we heard: *Let the Indians fend for themselves.* There had been five treaties between the US government and various tribes, including the Ponca, in which our people had been promised health care and education forever in exchange for millions of acres of our land. Chilocco's last superintendent was C. C. Tillman, a member of the Otoe-Missouria Tribe. In the school's 1980 yearbook, he wrote, "Chilocco is another in a long list of broken promises."

The BIA would be involved for a while, managing the grounds as a new regime took over. That new regime would be joint ownership of the school by five local tribes: Ponca, Kaw, Otoe-Missouria, Pawnee, and Tonkawa. They would comprise the Chilocco Development Authority. For the next forty years, the Authority would keep Chilocco's tree-lined grounds humming with various endeavors. It served as a substance abuse rehabilitation center, a law enforcement training center, a wind energy proving ground, a ranchland, and a homeland security testing site. The Cherokee Nation also had an interest in the Chilocco lands, but their deal was a little different, as it was their land before it was a school. They were given 2,500 acres on the east and west sides of the school. In addition to owning and running the school, the other five tribes were each given about 600 acres of land adjacent to the school.

Nearly 18,000 students from 126 Indian tribes had attended Chilocco. High school diplomas had been granted to 5,542 students, 2,741 young women and 2,801 young men. Graduates had included Cherokee, Choctaw, Creek, Kaw, Navajo, Otoe-Missouria, Pawnee, Ponca, Sioux, Tonkawa, and students from many more tribes. Even Alaskan Natives had been shipped south to attend the school. But putting them through the hot Oklahoma summers was cruel and dangerous to their health, so the government stopped that practice in the 1960s. Among all these Chilocco graduates had been four generations of my family. My aunt Tillie in fact was among the administrators who closed the school in 1980. Now it was my turn to go to Chilocco. I was already in my thirties. I had attended college and traveled extensively. I would go not as a student or a teacher. It would be a sad but necessary privilege to take part in the closing of this historic institution.

CHAPTER ELEVEN

My Chilocco Story

By the time I was old enough for school, my mother had decided to keep me close by instead of enrolling me in Chilocco like Donna, Mike, and Charmain. She sent me to the nearby grade school, and later, I attended the local high school. I learned white ways, but I also grew up embraced by my culture. As I neared the end of high school, I was a budding artist and story-teller, and I was ambitious. I wanted to go to college and was accepted into the University of Colorado Boulder. After two years, I set off on my own. It was the mid-1970s, and I had been inspired by the work of Clyde Warrior, my own Ponca brother. I was proud of my heritage, and I wanted to learn more about it and other American Indian cultures. My plan was to build a collection of American Indian tales. For the next five years, I traveled from coast to coast, collecting stories and interviews from many tribes before returning home.

Back at home in Oklahoma, I served my tribe as a council member in the late 1970s and early 1980s. During that time, I took part in Chilocco's closing. It was an organized government affair, led by professionals who knew how to proceed with shutting down a school. The US government held to their policy: If they had used lands that once belonged to Indian tribes, the tribes closest to the lands would receive them and everything on them. The lands, indeed, were returned. The BIA also stayed involved, working with the tribes to ensure an orderly closing. That included hiring maintenance staff.

After my term as council member was over, in 1984, I needed to work. So I contacted the local branch of the Bureau of Indian Affairs and asked to apply for any jobs they might have. I was told I could put in my application, but they didn't have any jobs I was qualified for. I guess they were thinking that after a college education and being a council member, I would only be interested in a desk job. I just happened to mention, "No jobs at all?" There was a long pause on the phone. "Well, Mr. Jones, I didn't mention we do have a maintenance job open."

"Maintenance?" I repeated. "Hmmm ... and where would that be?"

She was quick with her answer. "Chilocco."

I was just as quick to respond. "Oh my goodness, that sounds perfect," I said. "I've been cooped up in an office for the last four years." I filled out the application the following day.

A few weeks passed, and a letter came telling me I should report to the Bureau of Indian Affairs, Pawnee Agency, in Oklahoma, for orientation. It was all laid out in writing so there would be no mistakes or misunderstandings about any part of it. The job was maintenance and security of the Chilocco grounds and buildings. I would take daily orders from my supervisor to mow the grass, remove brush and plants that grew up around the buildings, maintain the water and electrical systems, and report any problems that needed professional attention. When the school was closed in 1980, the tools were stored in working condition, and we had access to those. If something went wrong and we couldn't fix it, we had a budget to call in service people. We were to maintain the roads and mend any breaks in the fences and gates surrounding Chilocco. We also were to follow security measures to keep unauthorized people out of the campus, especially the buildings.

Chilocco, abandoned.

The classrooms and other structures were getting old, and some were even dangerous. Most of the furniture and equipment had been removed from the buildings. It was sad to see what was once a bustling, working campus now sitting abandoned. Remember, this was not just a school but a small city and home to thousands of American Indians. Surrounding its lake were athletic fields, a swimming pool, a grand auditorium, vocational buildings, and a gas station. There was even a fully equipped fire station with two fire trucks called an assault vehicle and a ladder truck. There was a huge water tower eighty feet off the ground. We kept it filled by pumping from five wells that surrounded Chilocco.

Those five wells are still Chilocco's natural centerpiece. The school is famous for them. Called artesian springs, they are areas where pressure in the underground rocks forces water to flow up to the surface without needing a mechanical pump. Water even flows during severe droughts. In hard times, everyone knew Chilocco was the place to go for water. In good times, we might swim in the wells. Our tribes knew that Chilocco was once the site of an ancient Indian village, of the old people. They had lived here long before our people came to Oklahoma. They knew where to make a home!

There were three other employees at that time. The oldest gentleman was the supervisor. He was a member of the Yuccie people, a Nation that has long been within the jurisdiction of the Creek

Nation. The other two would be like me, just worker bees. One was a Navajo member. He was very interesting because he was adopted and raised by non-Indians, in the Ponca Area of Oklahoma. The other employee was a non-Indian man. They turned out to be a great group of government workers, and they took me right in.

Of Chilocco's 5,000 acres, the campus totaled 168 acres. That was the land we would be mowing. Two of us mowed on large, three-wheeled, three-bladed, hand-built mowers made in Kansas and called Heckendorn. One guy was on a tractor, pulling a brush hog. Starting at the Chilocco arch, it took us a week to mow the entire campus during peak mowing season. By the time we finished, the grass had grown and we had to start over. We all had a strong attachment to Chilocco. Generations of our families had either attended as students, or had worked there, or both. So doing a good job wasn't something we had to debate. It was just a given. We took our time, even using weed-eaters to get close to the fire hydrants and the corners of buildings where the big mowers couldn't reach.

One of the benefits of the job is that it came with a house on the grounds. No one was living there at this time, so I could have my choice. My girlfriend and I visited to make our selection. The visit was also an opportunity to show her what Chilocco meant to my family. I wanted her to understand the part it played in the nation's history. For me, it was a pilgrimage of sorts. As we drove toward the school, I pulled the truck over to the side of the road, right under the old arching sign, *Chilocco Indian Agricultural School*. Of the hundreds of times I had entered Chilocco, this was the first time I had stopped at the entrance. This sign was being constructed when my young grandmother arrived in 1884. It had towered over the entrance for a hundred years, a symbol of extreme sadness and great accomplishment.

What caught my eye next was a seven-foot-tall, rectangular granite stone supporting a bronze plaque, officially called the Cherokee Strip Marker. I knew it was a memorial to the Land Run of 1893. In that dark event for American Indians in Oklahoma and Kansas, the US government opened up millions of acres of Indian lands to anyone who was willing to race for it. I had never stopped to read the sign, because I was all too aware of the history behind it, and this sign added insult to injury. I very much resented it, but on this day, it felt different. As bad as this sign was, I wasn't going to change anything by not reading it. Erected in 1954 by the white women's organization the Colonial Dames, the sign read:

September 11, 1893: Thousands of Americans gathered in this township, preparing to make the run for homesteads in the Cherokee Strip, a tract of land 58 miles wide, opening 6,500,000 acres for white settlement bought from the Cherokee Nation by the U.S. government for $8,300,000 . . . At noon September 16, 1893, more than 100,000 people took part in this, the greatest race in the history of the world . . . Each settler paid about $2 an acre for his claim.

Historians have painted a pretty picture of the Land Run of 1893. They say it was an opportunity for people to own land and make new lives. In fact, it was a nightmare for thousands of people, a free-for-all in which American greed was set loose with minimal control. Like a mad-dash Black Friday sale, with people fighting and stomping on others to get the last on-sale products. The Oklahoma Land Run of 1893 was that, on steroids. Instead of a few hundred people at a single store, the Land Run was 100,000 people! Crazed for "free land."

Except, the land was stolen. The 6.5 million acres had been Cherokee land. The federal government had pressured the tribes to sell for a little more than $1 per acre. It was disgraceful. The Cherokee never wanted to sell, but they were between a rock and a hard place. If they refused, they knew the government would retaliate, perhaps simply taking the land with no payment at all. After signing the paperwork, the government took forever to pay the Cherokee. In the meantime, the United States made a huge profit by charging newcomers $2 an acre for the land. In addition, each new landowner had to pay $5 per acre in taxes within five years of buying the land. A similar scenario took place with the Pawnee and Tonkawa lands.

As the race loomed, fear filled the tribal communities. Chilocco, barely ten years old at the time, stood in the midst of the lineup of 100,000 people. This was simply another level of trauma for the children in the school (including my grandmother). Chilocco had all kinds of equipment and resources that unscrupulous runners could use for the race. Horses, wagons, tents, food, and more. Anticipating the violence to come, US soldiers ringed the school with bayonets affixed to their guns. The starting line extended as far as you could see, many lines deep with people and their modes of transportation.

On September 16, 1893, at high noon, the US Army cannons shook the earth with a loud report, followed by military rifles being shot, round after ear-splitting round. The race was on! The mass of humanity surged forward. They took off by horse, wagon, bicycle, surrey, and early automobile. My grandfather said one woman was riding a racehorse, a fine thoroughbred. (My grandfather also said she was later seen walking. She had run the horse to death in her rush to stake her claim.) Thousands of people walked. A few rode camels. The *Wichita Herald* reported that the government had commissioned freight trains to carry 2,000 passengers each. Some 20,000 attempted to board the lines. They crammed the corridors and clung to the train rooftops. Soldiers, land runners, and animals alike were trampled. Violence and greed ruled the day.

SOONERS AND BOOMERS

There turned out to be two types of people running for land, the Boomers and the Sooners. The Sooners did no running at all. Most were hard-core criminals, who were bad to the bone and had forged permits. They cheated their way into the race by sneaking across the border several days early and hiding from the military who were patrolling the lands for just such people. They could be shot on the spot if they tried to run from the soldiers. Boomers, on the other hand, played by the rules. They secured their official permits, and they lined up and waited for the cannons to blast on September 16 at high noon.

There were deadly conflicts long after the race ended. These were mainly due to the Sooners making false claims and Boomers challenging them later for the same claim. One such famous case was called the Lone Chimney Plot. A Boomer had claimed a 160-acre plot. The US government considered his claim fair (even though the claim was on stolen Pawnee lands!). He immediately started to build on this property. All he had constructed was the chimney to his new fireplace, when he had to go to town to get supplies. He did not know that a Sooner had staked a fake claim to the same property just days before. When the Boomer returned from his errand, he was met by the irate Sooner. After a heated argument, the Sooner pulled a revolver and shot the Boomer dead. This type of violence was taking place all over Indian Country. The Sooner was likely apprehended. The land was never developed. The unfinished fireplace still stands as a monument to greed.

After reading the plaque, I turned to my girlfriend and pointed across the highway to the empty lot where a small railroad station once stood. "Here," I told her, "Indian kids from across the country entered Chilocco." They'd arrive at the big railroad hub in Arkansas City, Kansas, about eight miles away. Then a short spur line would bring them to the school. Even more memorable was this: From the station in 1885, the renowned Nez Perce leader Chief Joseph was sent home from exile. He had been exiled near Chilocco next to the Ponca since 1878 for resisting the white man stealing and settling his Nez Perce lands in Oregon. When he was finally allowed to leave, his tribe's Oregon lands were all taken, so he was sent to Washington State. Chief Joseph's valor as a fierce

Chief Joseph.

leader and defender of his people would have inspired the children at Chilocco. But, in the early 1880s, the students would not have heard that story. They would have been taught only that the US Army had succeeded in quelling his uprising and in bringing peace to the land. Before Chief Joseph was released in 1885, he presented his hunting rifle to the school. My grandmother would have been four years old at the time, still at White Eagle School. The rifle was a .45 caliber made around 1860. Chief Joseph used it only for survival, to hunt for food during his years in exile. Chilocco's white administration would have enjoyed telling students that the revered Chief had been humbled. When Chilocco closed in 1980, the rifle was returned to Chief Joseph's Nez Perce descendants. His story has since been told.

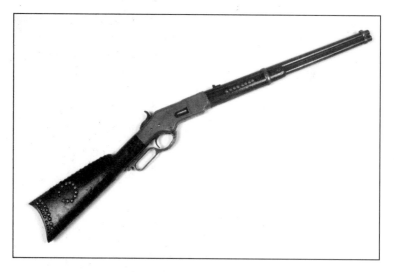

Chief Joseph's rifle.

CHIEF JOSEPH

Nez Perce Chief Joseph was the last great American Indian Chief to stand against white settlers as they swarmed to take his people's ancestral lands and burial grounds in the Wallowa Valley of today's Oregon. His band of Nez Perce Indians originated there, on the Pacific Coast. As his father lay dying in 1871, Joseph had promised he would defend the land, saying, "A man who would not love his father's grave is worse than a wild animal." Joseph and his people then set clear boundaries around their land and warned settlers not to trespass. But the settlers ignored them. Conflicts ensued.

Eventually, Joseph and his band were driven out by the US Army, toward a small reservation in Idaho. But the band detoured from the path commanded by the army. They traveled by foot through Wyoming and Montana Territory, planning to find refuge in Canada. Along the way they sought shelter with other tribes. No one would take them in. At last, they faced the US Army and fought. In the end, the army surrounded them and cut off their supplies. In freezing October snows of 1877, Joseph and his people were tired, starving, and dying of exposure. He surrendered. He spoke to US Army General Nelson Miles. "I am tired. My heart is sick and sad. From where the sun now stands, I shall fight no more forever!" Joseph was hailed by Indians and whites alike for his strength and bravery. Still, he and other leaders were incarcerated in 1878. For seven years, they survived in this unfamiliar territory, looking toward the day they could return home. In the end, they were sent to Washington State, because the white man had taken Nez Perce land.

Chief Joseph lived for nearly two decades more. He spoke out about the cruelty his people had suffered at the hands of the United States government, and he expressed his hope for equality for everyone, including American Indians.

At last, my girlfriend and I entered through the gates of Chilocco. The first thing I noticed was that the trees my grandmother had helped plant in the 1880s were dying. Many were already dead, and many more were on their way out. I couldn't help but see the irony of this. The trees died at the same time the school closed. No one could have planned that. The white man's grand vision had collapsed.

Our first choice for housing was to live in the old home of Superintendent Correll. That he had been a mentor to my sister Donna and her fellow students had meant a great deal to me. It was by far the nicest home at Chilocco. Solid stone and built to withstand even a tornado. But we met with a hiccup. The house had fallen into disrepair from the previous tenants. My new supervisor felt it was sacred ground and didn't want further disturbance. But I knew a few things about maintenance and explained that good occupants would keep the home breathing, so to speak. Warm in the winter and cool in the summer. Free of varmints that do a lot of damage. I told him we would clean it and fix it up and it would be as good as new, ready for another hundred years. He finally came around and assured me the shop had everything we needed to keep the place in great shape. So that was that. We would be moving into the Correll home after a full cleaning and painting. When we finished, I invited my boss over. The home was beautiful again, and he was pleased to see it. We were happy to respect the legacy of Superintendent Correll.

Then I got to work. With my colleagues, I mowed the grass in the spring, summer, and fall. In summer, we started early in the morning and stopped around noon for lunch. Then we worked in the shop or on campus doing whatever repairs were needed. Twice a day we'd take turns driving around the school's perimeter, making sure the fences and gates were all secure. On a couple of occasions, we discovered that someone had tried to drive a truck through one of the gates, only to find out how well built they were. It was obvious by the dent in the gate that they'd caused a good deal of damage to their truck.

I loved my job at Chilocco. My colleagues and I got along very well. We had the best equipment from Chilocco's former supplies. But it felt eerie sometimes, working in a place that was a ghost of its former self. I had arrived at Chilocco after it was picked apart. Once the BIA closed the school in 1980, they went about an orderly dismantling of the property. That included giving away all the equipment. The maintenance department had first choice. After that, the tribes came in to choose what they wanted. They took classroom desks, kitchen supplies, agricultural equipment including tractors, even a combine harvester worth $100,000. At last, representatives from the surrounding cities were allowed to come in and carry away whatever was left. The BIA offices there remained open to finalize the transfer of the property to the tribes, but the place was otherwise abandoned.

Yet Chilocco's spirit and the spirits of its students was pervasive. Even as a shell, Chilocco still breathed. It had stories to tell. Its grounds could be the foundation for inviting a greater understanding of American Indian Nations. I was an artist and a filmmaker, as a pastime, really. But I saw Chilocco as the place to tell important stories, not just about Chilocco and the American Indian boarding schools but about bigger issues: understanding American Indian heritage, our laws, and our interactions with white society. Such stories could answer questions most white Americans did not even know to ask.

I had been at Chilocco about a year, when I was able to talk the BIA officials into making a documentary on tribal sovereignty (the right of American Indians to govern their own tribes). The US Constitution indeed recognizes tribes as individual governments, with the same powers as federal and state government to regulate their affairs. The timing for such a topic was right. It had been more than a decade since the Termination Policy had been repealed in 1970. That policy had disbanded tribes and sold off even more of their land. Since its repeal, American Indians were working to reclaim their tribes and territories and heritage. I felt that greater white America's understanding of our freedom to govern ourselves was key to our future, especially those white communities surrounding tribal reservations. Many did not know the unique relationship that tribes have with the federal government. They didn't understand the treaties. Or why tribes don't adhere to state laws. Or why we have our own license plates. Or how we can run our own casinos outside of state control.

Working with a government expert on tribal sovereignty, I wrote the script for the short film titled *The Unique Relationship*. The film was narrated by William S. Banowsky, who was then president of Oklahoma University. When it came out, around 1985, this little film did a lot to increase understanding of our unique relationship with the US government. It was viewed mainly by government employees and was well received by them. In fact, they commended its content and clarity. This was the beginning of using Chilocco to reach the public. And my usefulness as a consultant had just increased.

Later, a producer and film director came to my tribe to let them know they were planning to do a film on our Ponca Chief Standing Bear. The tribe appointed me to work with them. The film was being made by NET, a television station in Lincoln, Nebraska, and would be aired in 1988 on the Public Broadcasting Service (PBS) as an episode of the long-standing program *Masterpiece Theater*. *The Trial of Standing Bear*, as it would be titled, would have a good budget. It sounded like the producer and director knew what they were doing. But they would need to cast actors for the movie and were looking for Oklahoma sites to film it in. I asked if they would like to see Chilocco. They loved it. Once again, I set up a meeting with the BIA officials, and it was a done deal. I was bringing another film to Chilocco! I also introduced the filmmakers to Wes Studi, a graduate of Chilocco. Because Wes is Cherokee, he is actually part owner of Chilocco. *The Trial of Standing Bear* was his first film. He had been in stage productions and was honing his craft. After this film, he went on to become an Academy

Award–winning actor with too many credits to mention. His blockbuster movies include *Avatar*, *The Last of the Mohicans*, and *Dances with Wolves*. I also introduced the filmmakers to my aunt Casey Camp-Horinek, of our Ponca tribe, an actress with scores of movie and television credits. She has as many connections to Chilocco as I have. There were many other American Indian actors, both male and female, who worked on this film early in their careers.

Chief Standing Bear.

Not long after the filming, the BIA would move out of the school completely, and the five tribes would take full control. As that day approached, the BIA started laying off the help. They terminated all the maintenance crew but me. They gave away the mowers and tractors and edging tools. They left one truck that I could use to patrol the grounds. I kept a fishing pole in the back. Nobody cared what I did. All they wanted was for me to be seen going in and out of the gates, maintaining some security. Members of the five tribes started coming around to walk the property. I would give them tours, to show what was working and what was not. I knew I was about to lose my government job at Chilocco, but, technically, I would not be gone. My tribe was one of the five tribes about to take control of the school. I would be valuable to them all. The campus was no small place, and I knew the ins and outs of its many systems.

At last, the end was here. It was 1985. We planned a weekend-long celebration of religious ceremonies and dances, with lots of food for all the members of the five tribes. Living at Chilocco, I was a member of the Powwow Committee. I had become friends with the big ranchers who leased Chilocco lands, so I asked for donations for our celebration. That meant cattle. In our heritage, we want to know the origin of the meat we eat. It is important for our children to know where their food comes from. This is especially important for such a celebration. The ranchers gifted us two cows. As is our custom, we butchered them on the morning of the celebration, to enjoy the meat in its freshest state. It was a pretty remarkable weekend. The tribes did it right. Here we were, descendants of loved ones who had attended Chilocco for over a century. We were dancing and singing in our languages, in a place that had tried to take those customs away. We were praying in honor of ancestors who had felt fear, loneliness, hunger, and punishment. But also for those who had experienced happiness, love, laughter, and success. All the students at Chilocco had paved the way for our tribes to protect our heritage and share it with future generations. Here we were now, celebrating their resilience.

It was time for my girlfriend and me to move on. And we did. For a while I lived in Santa Monica, California, working for Disney as an honorary Imagineer. That was cool. Finally, I made a film for NBC titled *The World of American Indian Dance*. After a while, I decided to go back home to Oklahoma and get back into politics. I became the Chairman of the Ponca Nation. I also worked more frequently as a sculptor, creating artwork that represented our tribe and its history and stories. During all the years, memories of Chilocco had stayed with me.

Around 2019, the Kaw Nation contacted me and said they wanted a monument at the Chilocco cemetery in remembrance of all the children who died there before 1935. Those children were buried there, never to see their homes or family again. I told them I would be honored to build it and would put some concept designs together for them to pick what they wanted. They didn't have a huge budget, but I was intent on doing the monument if I had to pay for it myself. They chose one of the designs, and I set off to build it. When I finished, they were very impressed. Then came time to install the monument. A crew from the Tonkawa tribe was helping me pour the cement base we'd set the monument on. When I pour a base, I generally stay with it until it is dry, so nothing happens to it. But we finished late that evening, and everyone wanted to go home. So did I.

That night I had the most visual dream I can remember. We were working in the cemetery, and it was very foggy. A young boy, fifteen or sixteen years old, was walking through the fog. He was carrying an infant. He began speaking to me in a language I didn't understand. I asked him if he was lost. "There is no one at the school anymore," I told him. "You must not be from around here."

He responded to me in clear English. "No, I take care of the children," he said. "There is no one to take care of them anymore."

As he spoke, little children began walking out of the fog. They gathered around the boy and looked up at me. I realized I was in a dream. I was talking to a ghost. I woke up with a start.

When I got to the cemetery the next morning, the Tonkawa crew was there. But instead of preparing to install the monument, they were all sitting in their truck. It looked like they were getting ready to leave.

The monument for the children who died and were buried at Chilocco.

"What's wrong?" I asked the foreman.

"You need to look at that pad we poured last night," he said.

I walked over to it and looked in disbelief. Someone, or more than one person, had played in the wet concrete. Foot- and handprints were all over it. It was completely destroyed. Then I remembered my dream.

The foreman spoke again. "My crew don't want to work here. They want to get out of here as soon as possible."

I looked again at the slab, then I laughed. Those weren't human prints. "A couple of raccoons had fun in our wet concrete last night," I told the foreman. "Get those boys over here, and let's tear this out before it gets any harder."

But that dream stayed with me. We soon completed the memorial statue, and it was blessed in a moving ceremony in June 2022. Its stone slab bears the names of sixty-seven children, representing seventy-nine tribes. Their remains were identified in the cemetery using ground-penetrating radar. Situated at the entrance to the Chilocco cemetery, near Takare's grave, I think of the statue as watching over Takare and the other children who died so far from home of disease, of drowning, and of broken hearts. Like the young boy in my dream, the monument reminds us that we will always watch over the children, to take care of them.

CHAPTER TWELVE

Let the Truth-Telling Begin

Today, Chilocco is a ruin. Some buildings have collapsed. Others are structurally unsound and dangerous to enter. The grounds are overgrown. "It grieves my soul to see the place like this," Claudine King told a National Public Radio reporter in 2021.

Claudine, a 1952 graduate of Chilocco, is a member of an alumni group that still gathers to share their stories and honor Chilocco's past. Claudine, along with my sister Charmain and her husband, Jim Baker, all worked at the school and witnessed its closing from 1980–1985 and its years of silence. Still, they maintained ties with other alumni from more than 127 tribes and kept the memory of Chilocco alive. From 2016 to 2018, Charmain, Jim, Claudine, and others in the Chilocco National Alumni Association partnered with Oklahoma State University to carry out the Chilocco History Project. Through it, forty-four alumni have recorded their memories. Generations to come will hear their stories.

While Chilocco experienced several lives after closing, other boarding schools saw varied change. Some, like Mount Pleasant Indian School in Saginaw, Michigan, and Genoa

Charmain and Jim Baker.

Indian Industrial School in Nebraska, were closed and abandoned or demolished soon after the Meriam Report of 1928 exposed heinous crimes against children. Some, like Haskell Institute in Kansas, and Phoenix Indian School in Arizona, were repurposed. Since 1993, Haskell has been an Indian Nations University. Phoenix gradually was turned into a park and visitor center, with plans for a museum.

A handful of schools, like Chemawa, remained open, run by the Bureau of Indian Affairs. Gradually, those schools incorporated Native languages, cultures, and traditions into their curriculum. Chemawa's buildings were demolished in the 1990s and a new campus was built, but the school remains under white control. Still other schools, such as Rainy Mountain in Oklahoma, fell to ruin. Despite their conditions, the schools were sacred places, time capsules for the spirits and remains of the children buried there. For decades, beyond the children's families and tribes, little attention was paid to finding their remains and memorializing their lives.

As boarding schools closed and reinvented themselves in the 1980s and 1990s, United States policy toward Indian Nations seemed to be moving in a positive direction. In 1983, President Ronald Reagan acknowledged the government-to-government relationship between the United States and Indian Nations. He confirmed the policy of tribal sovereignty proposed by President Richard Nixon in the 1970s. Subsequent presidents have echoed this support. In 1984, the Environmental Protection Agency (EPA) announced policies to benefit our land and people. In 1990, Congress passed the Native American Grave Protection and Repatriation Act to guard Native burial grounds on federal lands and to return the remains to families. All of these policies are good. But with no tribal voice in Washington, the seat of government, actual enactment of them was slow.

At last, in 2009, President Barack Obama announced the opening of the Embassy of Tribal Nations in Washington, DC. This is the headquarters for the National Congress of American Indians (NCAI). Here, leaders from across the Indian Nations can gather to share their vision and plans, and to work directly with members of the US Congress and government departments to take action on important policies. Gradually, ties are strengthening between the US and tribal governments. In 2010, Congress passed the Indian Health Care Improvement Act. In 2011, the NCAI took on an international role, collaborating with Indigenous peoples around the world.

Still, our stolen lands have not been returned. The Department of the Interior has long kept 56 million acres in a "land trust." That means they are holding the land "for the benefit of a tribe or individual tribal members." Lands placed in a trust are said to receive tax credits and allow other benefits to a tribe. But we are not allowed to even have a say in how the lands are controlled and cared for.

Then, a breakthrough came in 2016, again under President Barack Obama. He accepted a proposal by five tribes, the Hopi, Navajo, Zuni, Ute, and Ute Mountain Ute people. They wanted to protect 1.35 million acres of their ancestral land in Utah. Obama soon issued a Presidential Proclamation for that area, to "preserve its landscape and unique cultural resources." The area is now known as the Bears Ears National Monument. At the same time, he named the five tribes as the Bears Ears Commission, to guide the government's management of the monument. For the first time since the United States took our lands, American Indians had been given a voice in how some of the lands would be controlled.

A setback occurred in 2017 during the administration of President Donald Trump. Not only was 85 percent of Bears Ears land revoked, but EPA regulations were ignored. The NCAI had little interaction with the government. In 2021, under President Joseph Biden's administration, the lands were returned. Our voices again were heard.

While the greater Indian-US policies have been improving and boarding schools have been closing since the 1980s, a pall still settled over thousands of American Indian families. The memories held by students who had suffered boarding school abuse remained. They were now parents and grandparents, and they were abusing their own children as they had once been abused. They were not alumni like Claudine, Charmain, and Jim, who valued their Chilocco experiences and passed on good memories to their children. They were the survivors who had been physically and verbally punished. They passed on their suffering to the next generation. At the same time, that new generation was working to reclaim the culture and values their parents had lost during the era.

Denise K. Lajimodiere is part of that next generation. As a direct descendant of boarding school survivors, she has felt the long-term effects of the boarding school era. She and others like her experience what is called intergenerational trauma. That is why she has dedicated her life to healing and to helping others heal. She started her work at home, on a personal level with her family. In the 1980s and 1990s, she recorded her grandfather's stories, then her father's. Around 2008, she started recording other survivors' stories. "I've learned that talking about their experiences can help boarding school survivors heal from their trauma," she says.

Denise's work expanded in 2011, when she and others cofounded the National Native American Boarding School Healing Coalition (NABS). As a researcher and tenure-track professor in Educational Leadership at North Dakota State University, she embraced her work in the organization. By 2023, NABS members were using their voice—a coalition of over 800

Denise K. Lajimodiere's grandfather and his sister at Fort Totten Boarding School.

NATIONAL NATIVE AMERICAN BOARDING SCHOOL HEALING COALITION

The National Native American Boarding School Healing Coalition, or NABS, began in 2001 as the National Boarding School Healing Project. It was the idea of Samantha Toineeta, a member of the Rosebud Sioux Tribe of South Dakota and a boarding school survivor. Samantha sought advice and direction from leaders of other groups healing from trauma. Together, the groups created a task force on boarding schools. They had learned that many survivors suffered trauma while retelling their stories and needed therapy afterward. So the task force determined a safe and effective protocol for helping survivors tell their stories in a respectful and private environment. In 2010, Denise K. Lajimodiere reached out to the project after reading about it in a magazine article. "They were seeking Native researchers to interview survivors, documenting human rights abuses," she said. "I had already been interviewing my family, so I volunteered."

Denise was not alone in working on boarding school issues—other groups were doing similar work across the United States and Canada. Several groups formed an alliance and decided to name it the National Native American Boarding School Healing Coalition. The acronym included the word *nabs*, a reference to Native children literally being nabbed and stolen from homes during the boarding school era. The NABS mission is to educate government agencies and churches about the boarding school era and its impact. To help individuals, families, communities, and Tribal Nations who were victims of the era, to seek meaningful compensation, or redress. And to support lasting and true community-directed healing.

individuals—to educate others about the truth of the federal Indian boarding school era in both its historical and contemporary impacts.

Today, NABS calls for action toward justice. It uses its network to engage in research and healing for survivors. It presses the US Congress to officially declare these wrongs and make reparations, or amends. During its first ten years, from 2011 to 2021, NABS worked hard to bring the horrors of the boarding school era to Congress and the nation. But there was little traction.

Then something extraordinary happened that brought national attention overnight.

In late May 2021, the Kamloops First Nation released the findings of ground-penetrating radar (GPR) at the former Kamloops Indian Residential School, in British Columbia, Canada. The school had operated from 1890 until the late 1970s. The radar showed the presence of 215 unmarked graves of children who had died at the school. Some graves were tiny, holding the remains of children as young as three years old. The findings shook Native Nations across Canada, and made news throughout Canada, the United States, and around the world.

News media soon reached out to Denise and others in the United States who were involved in boarding school research. Reporters had read Denise's 2019 book *Stringing Rosaries*, a series of interviews with boarding school survivors. "I repeatedly told them it was America's best-kept secret," says Denise. "Boarding school history was never written into history books." Generally, survivors have never had a forum or a means to tell their story. When they do, they must be supported by family or therapists, or spiritual healers.

Not long after the Kamloops story came to light, American Indian Nations received an advocate like none they had ever had. And she moved fast. On March 16, 2021, Deb Haaland, a member of the Pueblo of Laguna, New Mexico, became the first Native American to serve in a US presidential cabinet. Appointed by

President Joseph Biden, she is serving as the fifty-fourth United States secretary of the Interior. It is the Department of the Interior, with its Bureau of Indian Affairs, that was responsible for establishing and running most of the American Indian boarding schools.

Just three months after she entered office, on June 22, 2021, Secretary Haaland directed Department of the Interior agencies to coordinate an investigation into the federal Indian boarding school system. The agencies were to examine the scope of the system and to identify the location of the schools, their burial sites, and the children who attended the schools.

US Secretary of the Interior Deb Haaland.

DEB HAALAND, US SECRETARY OF
THE INTERIOR

Secretary of the Interior Deb Haaland knows the meaning of hardship. Her grandparents were boarding school survivors. Her brilliant grandfather, a musician and master of languages, had little choice but to spend a career as a diesel mechanic. With limited income, he raised his family in a boxcar. Deb's own parents raised her in a loving home, where she learned pride in her heritage and self-confidence. But it wasn't easy. Her white father, a decorated Vietnam War veteran and career marine, was often transferred. Deb attended thirteen schools before graduating high school. College was expensive, but Deb was determined. She developed her own business producing salsa and saved enough to start college at the age of twenty-eight. Not long after graduating, she became a single mother who worked while raising her child. There were times when she had no more than $5 in her bank account. Times when she had to decide between paying rent and buying groceries for her child. But it didn't keep her down.

Soon she earned a law degree. She took on leadership roles in her tribe and community. National politics followed. In 2019, the US Congress welcomed Deb and Sharice Davids, of the Ho-Chunk tribe, as the first American Indian women ever to serve as US representatives. Deb was poised to make an even greater impact in her appointment as secretary of the Interior. The Department of the Interior's mandate has long included managing all of America's natural resources and cultural heritage. Immediately, she formed task forces to address land and water health, climate change, and the energy crisis. She revoked policies that ignored science and harmed the health of people, wildlands, and wildlife. She put her commitment to the Bureau of Indian Affairs on high speed.

Less than a year later, on May 11, 2022, the final report, titled *Federal Indian Boarding School Initiative Investigative Report*, was submitted by Assistant Secretary of Indian Affairs Bryan Newland. The report shows that between 1819 and 1969, the United States operated or supported 408 boarding schools across 37 states (or then-territories), including 21 schools in

Alaska and 7 schools in Hawaii. The report also identified fifty-three burial sites. More site discoveries and data are expected as the research continues. The schools with burial sites have not been released. As soon as the report was published, Secretary Haaland immediately launched her Road to Healing initiative. She and Assistant Secretary Newland spent a year traveling across the nation to hear for themselves the stories of survivors. In school gyms and churches and tribal centers around the country, they listened as boarding school survivors testified to their unspeakable experiences, vowing that

Map of residential boarding school sites identified by the Federal Indian Boarding School Initiative at the Department of the Interior.

FEDERAL INDIAN BOARDING SCHOOL INITIATIVE INVESTIGATIVE REPORT

With Assistant Secretary of Indian Affairs Bryan Newland, of the Bay Mills Ojibwe community, Secretary of the Interior Deb Haaland led a powerful nationwide effort to bring the injustices and horrors of American Indian boarding schools to light. After the investigations, they released a 100-page report highlighting the schools' "rampant physical, sexual, and emotional abuse." The report explored multiple aspects of the schools across the United States, including in Alaska and Hawaii. These are the key recommendations for next steps.

- Determine the number of children, from which tribes, were sent to the schools.
- Locate all burial sites and names of the children, with their tribes, buried there.
- Build a database of school profiles and histories, to create a complete picture.
- List the diseases and deaths of students, to understand school health care practices.

- Document the government financial aid sent to the schools; was it properly used?
- Identify state governments, schools, and other institutions that received funds meant to support the schools.
- Identify adoption and foster care programs that, in addition to the boarding schools, removed children from their homes.
- Develop a central Department of the Interior archive for all boarding school records.
- Allow tribes to reclaim all former boarding school sites or co-manage them with the US government.
- Fund language programs for all Nations, to revitalize that key element of their heritage.

Soon after the report was released, Secretary Haaland spoke out about the healing work that lies ahead. "I know this process will be long and difficult. I know that this process will be painful. It won't undo the heartbreak and loss we feel. But only by acknowledging the past can we work toward a future that we're all proud to embrace."

these tragedies will not be repeated. In July 2023, at the former Riverside Indian School in Oklahoma, Secretary Haaland held back tears as members of the Caddo, Delaware, and Wichita tribes shared their stories. "I will listen with you, I will grieve with you, I will weep and I will feel your pain as we mourn what we have lost," she told them. "Please know that we still have so much to gain. The healing that can help our communities will not be done overnight, but it will be done."

While the investigative report was being compiled, Senator Elizabeth Warren of Massachusetts and the US Senate Committee on Indian Affairs introduced a new bill to Congress in September 2021. It would establish a Truth and Healing Commission on Indian boarding school policies in the United States. Among other duties, the commission would investigate the impacts and ongoing effects of the Indian boarding school policies started in the 1800s. Further, the commission would recommend ways to bring justice to Tribal Nations through reparations.

Three kinds of reparations are a priority. First, children's unmarked graves and the land around them must be protected. Second, the Tribal Nations of the deceased children must be identified and the children's remains returned to their homelands. Finally, any removal of American Indian, Alaska Native, and Native Hawaiian children from their families and tribal

Student grave at St. Boniface Indian Industrial Boarding School.

communities must never happen again. That means no state social service departments, foster care agencies, adoption agencies, or other groups can ever again take an Indian child from their home.

The bill to establish the Truth and Healing Commission has seen significant momentum since it was introduced in 2021. As of 2024, the bill was still being considered. Hopes remain high that it will soon be passed. NABS members have contributed greatly to the language of the bill. They have educated Congress on the history of boarding school trauma and its impacts passed from generation to generation. And they continue a national advocacy campaign, making the public aware of the bill and pushing Congress to pass it. Support is rising. NABS has gained twenty-six co-sponsors in the Senate and eighty-seven co-sponsors in the House. Two congressional hearings have further advanced public awareness of boarding schools.

"I am saddened," says Denise K. Lajimodiere, "that it took national and international news of the unmarked graves at Kamloops Indian Residential School, in Canada, to bring attention to our own United States boarding school era. Through my years of research, I know that there are many unmarked graves at schools across the United States."

Those include the graves at Chemawa, the school where Denise's father spent hard years. Long before the historic campus was razed in the 1990s, the cemetery was leveled in 1960. The grave markers were also destroyed or lost. Over decades,

Graves of Native students at the Carlisle Indian Industrial School.

families, teachers, students, and local tribes worked to identify the children buried there. They used an old map of the cemetery and matched the grave sites to student records of deaths and burials from the National Archives and Records office in Seattle. At last, on Indigenous Peoples' Day, October 11, 2021, "Deaths at Chemawa" was published online, with records dating to 1881. It included a spreadsheet that put as many names as possible to the small graves. Those children's final resting place was finally known.

How many boarding schools have existed across the United States? Where are they located? How many students attended each one? How many died? What were their causes of death? How many are buried at the schools, never to return? Can students buried at these boarding schools be repatriated, meaning returned to their families and tribes? With NABS working closely with Congress and Secretary Deb Haaland to pass the Truth and Healing Commission bill, those questions may soon be answered.

Says Denise, "Let the truth-telling begin."

That truth-telling was at the heart of the Chilocco Alumni gathering when the former students came together in 2021. They reminisced. They told stories. They laughed. They also acknowledged what had come before them. Early students had suffered here, and trauma was great. Slowly, the group rose from their gathering beneath the trees and walked across the grounds, over

Chilocco Creek bridge. They made their way through a field of shoulder-high grass. Without a word they entered the gate of Chilocco cemetery. Here, my sister Charmain greeted the children laid to rest under soil and grass so many years before, including the first in 1884, Takare of the Wichita Indian Tribe.

Charmain's eyes filled with tears as she spoke of the children's fears at being far from home, isolated, thrust into an environment with alien languages, customs, and rules. They became ill without loving parents to care for them. Charmain has worked to identify these unknown children. At the National Archives, in Washington, DC, she found the government letters sent home to parents whose children had died. "One letter said the child had suffered so much that death came as a relief," Charmain recalled. Many of the grave markers had no more than a first name. No last name. No tribe. No date. "The disrespect for our children," she said, "is just incomprehensible."

Her search to identify them and honor them continues. With her husband, Jim; her friend Claudine; and their fellow alumni, Charmain has made a commitment, one that is echoed across the nation. The children buried here will not be forgotten.

CONCLUSION

I look back on my days charged with maintaining Chilocco Indian Agricultural School after it closed. My responsibility was to oversee a decaying empire. Houses moldering and rotting, with no staff to bring them heat and life and to arrest the ruin. Huge buildings with Nature clawing at them, first by sending vines and saplings slowly but surely to wrap and strangle the foundations, cracking and breaking them apart. Then by sending bird after bird on a suicidal mission to fly full speed into one of the windows, breaking out the glass while ending its tiny life. Through that break more of Nature would creep to destroy more of the building. Rain and seeds blew in. Gradually, an environment of its own took root in the linoleum floor, soon rich with growing and creeping things.

We three last caretakers ran around trying to stop Nature's slow destruction as we cut and pulled fledgling trees from the buildings' bases. We repaired the bird-shattered windows until we ran out of glass. The BIA would not approve the purchase of new panes. No budget, they said. So, we cut plywood boards and stuck them into place to stop what was unstoppable.

I was watching the death of a being. Despite the stories of hardship some students suffered there, that being had sheltered and raised many of my family members. At the time when Chilocco was vitally alive, hundreds of people had watched over her. Now there were just three of us, and we were losing badly.

Today, in the 2020s, I visit the grounds and I know that Nature has won. Just as the government had designed this place to destroy our culture, once we made a success of the school and its students, the government let Chilocco slip into obscurity along with the philosophy that started it all: "Kill the Indian in him, and save the man." Let it all just go away.

Perhaps American Indians can make no great statement to the world that we are here to stay. But we are people who defend our culture, and we will find the way to live on. I used to think there was an urgency to secure our future, and that the buildings were an important part of that security. I have pondered how to do this, and I have thought that we could turn Chilocco into a great statement, a national center for preserving American Indian culture. But I realize that is not the case.

We are more like the land than the buildings. The land will always be there, where generations of our people have lived and made a difference and left a part of themselves. The land can never be forgotten, covered up, or destroyed. Its stories can never die. So, in the end, it is not the buildings that will allow our people to live on, but Nature's unstoppable quest to take back our land. That is the American Indian's best hope for the future.

BIBLIOGRAPHY

Books

Adams, David Wallace. *Education for Extinction: American Indians and the Boarding School Experience, 1875–1928*. Lawrence, KS: University of Kansas Press, 2020.

Bloom, John. *To Show What an Indian Can Do: Sports at Native American Boarding Schools*. Minneapolis, MN: University of Minnesota Press, 2000.

Fear-Segal, Jacqueline, and Susan D. Rose, eds. *Carlisle Industrial School: Indigenous Histories, Memories, and Reclamations*. Lincoln, NE: University of Nebraska Press, 2016.

Gale Research, Inc. *Encyclopedia of World Biography*. Farmington Hills, MI: Gale; 2nd edition, 2014.

Grann, David. *Killers of the Flower Moon: The Osage Murders and the Birth of the FBI*. New York: Doubleday, 2017.

Howard, James H. *The Ponca Tribe*. Smithsonian Institution Bureau of American Ethnology, Bulletin 195. Washington, DC: US Government Printing Office, 1965.

Kortenhof, Kurt, *Fight No More: Episodes of Conflict in the Trans-Mississippi West, 1862–1890*, "Chief Joseph: Good Words." Minneapolis, MN: Minnesota Libraries Publications Project, University of Minnesota, 2023. https://mlpp.pressbooks.pub/woundedknee/.

La Flesche, Francis, *The Middle Five: Indian Boys at School*. Boston, MA: Small, Maynard & Company, 1909. https://www.gutenberg.org/ebooks/62094.

Lajimodiere, Denise K. *Bitter Tears*. Lawrence, KS: Mammoth Publications, 2016.

———. *Stringing Rosaries: The History, the Unforgivable, and the Healing of Northern Plains American Indian Boarding School Survivors*. Fargo, ND: North Dakota State University Press, 2021.

Lomawaima, K. Tsianina. *They Called It Prairie Light: The Story of Chilocco Indian School*. Lincoln, NE: University of Nebraska Press, 1995.

O'Brien, Cynthia. *National Geographic Kids Encyclopedia of American Indian History and Culture: Stories, Timelines, Maps, and More*. Washington, DC: National Geographic Society, 2019.

Pearson-Little Thunder, Julie; Johnnie Diacon; Jerry Bennett. *Chilocco Indian School: A Generational Story*. Stillwater, OK: Oklahoma State University Library. *Chilocco History Project, 2022*. https://chilocco.library.okstate.edu/items/show/3867.

Peavy, Linda, and Ursula Smith. *Full-Court Quest: The Girls from Fort Shaw Indian School, Basketball Champions of the World*. Norman, OK: University of Oklahoma Press, 2008.

Sasakamoose, Fred. *Call Me Indian: From the Trauma of Residential School to Becoming the NHL's First Treaty Indigenous Player*. New York: Viking, 2021.

Standing Bear, Luther. *Land of the Spotted Eagle*. Lincoln, NE: Bison Books, University of Nebraska Press, 2006.

Trafzer, Clifford E.; Jean A. Keller; Lorene Sisquoc, eds. *Boarding School Blues: Revisiting American Indian Educational Experiences*. Lincoln, NE: University of Nebraska Press, 2006.

Viola, Herman J. *Warrior Spirit: The Story of Native American Patriotism and Heroism*. Norman, OK: University of Oklahoma Press, 2022.

Encyclopedia Articles

Encyclopedia.com. "American Indians 1933–1941." https://www.encyclopedia.com/education/news-and-education-magazines/american-indians-1933-1941.

———. "John Collier." https://www.encyclopedia.com/people/social
-sciences-and-law/sociology-biographies/john-collier.

———. "Native Americans, Impact of the Great Depression On." https://
www.encyclopedia.com/economics/encyclopedias-almanacs
-transcripts-and-maps/native-americans-impact-great-depression.

Gunn, Steven J. "Indian General Allotment Act (Dawes Act)
(1887)." Encyclopedia.com. https://www.encyclopedia.com
/history/encyclopedias-almanacs-transcripts-and-maps
/indian-general-allotment-act-dawes-act-1887.

Patterson, Sara M. "Indian Removal Act (1830)." Encyclopedia.com. https://
www.encyclopedia.com/history/united-states-and-canada/north
-american-indigenous-peoples/indian-removal-act.

Westmoreland, Ingrid P. "Nez Perce." Encyclopedia of Oklahoma History
and Culture. https://www.okhistory.org/publications/enc/entry.php
?entry=NE015.

Magazine and Newspaper Articles

Bear, Charla. "American Indian Boarding Schools Haunt Many." *Morning
Edition.* NPR, May 12, 2008. https://www.npr.org/2008/05/12/16516865
/american-indian-boarding-schools-haunt-many.

Blakemore, Erin. "What Really Happened at Wounded Knee, the Site
of a Historic Massacre." *National Geographic*, November 19, 2021.
https://www.nationalgeographic.com/history/article/what-really
-happened-at-wounded-knee-the-site-of-a-historic-massacre.

Breda, Isabelle. "Tulalip's Stolen Children." *Daily Herald*, June 2022. https://
www.heraldnet.com/native-boarding-schools/.

Brewer, Graham Lee. "Indian Boarding School Investigation Faces
Hurdles in Missing Records, Legal Questions." *NBC News*,
July 15, 2021. https://www.nbcnews.com/news/us-news

/indian-boarding-school-investigation-faces-hurdles-missing-records
-legal-questions-n1273996.

Brice, Anne. "How the U.S. Government Created an 'Insane
Asylum' to Imprison Native Americans." Berkeley News,
November 19, 2020. https://news.berkeley.edu/2020/11/19
/using-disability-to-imprison-native-americans/.

Brown, Matthew. "Survivors Tell Grim Stories of Boarding
School Experiences." Associated Press, reprinted in *Indian
Country Today*. October 15, 2022. https://ictnews.org/news
/survivors-tell-grim-stories-of-boarding-school-experiences.

Fife, Ari. "At One Former Native American School in Oklahoma, Honoring
the Dead Now Falls to Alumni." *The Frontier*, July 21, 2021. https://
www.readfrontier.org/stories/at-one-former-native-american
-school-in-oklahoma-honoring-the-dead-now-falls-to-alumni/.

Gerian, Charles. "Chilocco Part 1: Alumni Fondly Recall School
Days." *Blackwell Journal-Tribune*, reprinted in the *Native News
Online*. July 30, 2021. https://nativenewsonline.net/currents
/chilocco-part-1-alumni-fondly-recall-school-days.

———. "Chilocco Part 2: "Medals of Honor, the '55 Tornado, and
Misguided Beginnings." *Blackwell Journal-Tribune*, reprinted in
the *Native News Online*. July 31, 2021. https://nativenewsonline.net
/currents/chilocco-part-2-medals-of-honor-the-55-tornado-and
-misguided-beginnings.

———. "Chilocco Part 3: Life, Legacy, and Heritage," *Blackwell
Journal-Tribune*, reprinted in the *Native News Online*.
August 1, 2021. https://nativenewsonline.net/currents
/chilocco-part-3-life-legacy-and-heritage.

Heller, Karen. "Interior Secretary Deb Haaland's Charged Mission of
Healing." *Washington Post*, July 17, 2023. https://www.washingtonpost
.com/lifestyle/2023/07/17/deb-haaland-road-to-healing/.

Herrera, Allison. "Chilocco Indian Agricultural School Should Remain 'A Site of Conscience.'" NPR KOSU in production with Newsy's In Real Life and Fire Thief Production, December 21, 2021. https://www.kosu .org/history/2021-12-21/chilocco-indian-agricultural-school-should -remain-site-of-conscience.

Manning, Rob. "Interior Department leaders decry traumatic legacy of federal boarding schools for Native American children." Oregon Public Broadcasting, May 11, 2022. https://www.opb.org/article/2022/05/11 /interior-department-leaders-decry-traumatic-legacy-native-american -boarding-schools/.

Mansky, Jackie. "The True Story of Pocahontas." *Smithsonian*, March 23, 2017. https://www.smithsonianmag.com/history /true-story-pocahontas-180962649/.

Pate, Natalie; Capi Lynn; and Dianne Lugo. "Chemawa Indian School Families Seek Answers, Healing Through Federal Investigation." *Salem Statesmen Journal* and *USA Today*. October 24, 2021. (Updated October 26, 2021.) https://www.usatoday.com/in-depth/news/nation /2021/10/24/native-american-assimilation-boarding-schools-chemawa -salem-oregon-deb-haaland/6165318001/.

Pember, Mary Annette. "Death by Civilization." *The Atlantic,* March 8, 2019. https://www.theatlantic.com/education/archive/2019/03/traumatic -legacy-indian-boarding-schools/584293/.

———. "Indian Assimilation: The Mystery of the Tiny Handcuffs, Solved." *Indian Country Today*, September, 12, 2018. https://ictnews.org/archive /indian-assimilation-the-mystery-of-the-tiny-handcuffs-solved.

Wagner, Kelsey. "146th Annual Ponca Tribal Celebration." *Ponca City Monthly*, August 1, 2022. https://poncacitymonthly.com/articles/146th -annual-ponca-tribal-celebration/19027/.

Walker, David Edward. "A Living Burial: Inside Hiawatha Asylum for Insane Indians." *Indian Country Today*, November 9, 2015. (Updated

September 13, 2018.) https://ictnews.org/archive
/a-living-burial-inside-the-hiawatha-asylum-for-insane-indians.

Young, Brian. "Why I Won't Wear War Paint and Feathers in a Movie
Again." *Zocalo Public Square*, reprinted *Time.* June 11, 2015. https://time
.com/3916680/native-american-hollywood-film/.

Journal Articles, Periodicals, and Reports

Boxer, Andrew. "Native Americans and the Federal Government." *History
Review*, issue 64 (September 2009). https://www.historytoday.com
/archive/feature/native-americans-and-federal-government.

Crowe, F. Hilton. "Indian Prisoner-Students at Fort Marion: The Founding
of Carlisle Was Dreamed in St. Augustine." *The Regional Review*, vol. 5,
no. 6. US (December 1940). https://www.nps.gov/parkhistory/online
_books/regional_review/vol5-6c.htm.

"Healing Voices: A Primer on American Indian and Alaska Native Boarding
Schools in the U.S." National Native American Boarding
School Healing Coalition, 2nd edition (June 2020). https://
boardingschoolhealing.org/wp-content/uploads/2021/09/NABS
-Newsletter-2020-7-1-spreads.pdf.

Jones, Paul Mckenzie. "'We are among the poor, the powerless, the inex-
perienced and the inarticulate': Clyde Warrior's Campaign for a
'Greater Indian America.'" *The American Indian Quarterly*, vol. 34, no. 2
(Spring 2010). https://go.gale.com/ps/i.do?p=LitRC&u=new80463&id=
GALE|A224167270&v=2.1&it=r&sid=googleScholar&asid=b506af69.

Lough, Jean C. "Gateways to the Promised Land: The Role Played by the
Southern Kansas Towns in the Opening of the Cherokee Strip to
Settlement." *The Kansas Historical Quarterly*, vol. 25, no. 1 (Spring 1959).
https://www.kshs.org/p/gateways-to-the-promised-land/13149.

McKinney, Lillie G. "History of Albuquerque Indian School (to 1934)," *New Mexico Historical Review*, vol. 20, no. 4. (1945). https://digitalrepository .unm.edu/nmhr/vol20/iss4/3.

Reyhner, Jon. "American Indian Boarding Schools: What Went Wrong? What Is Going Right?" *Journal of American Indian Education*, vol. 57, no. 1 (Spring 1918). https://www.jstor.org/stable/10.5749 /jamerindieduc.57.1.0058.

Press Releases

Department of the Interior. "Department of the Interior Releases Investigative Report, Outlines Next Steps in Federal Indian Boarding School Initiative." May 11, 2022. https://www.doi.gov/pressreleases /department-interior-releases-investigative-report-outlines-next-steps -federal-indian.

Websites and Blogs

Access Genealogy. "Chilocco Indian School Records 1884–1980." https:// accessgenealogy.com/native/chilocco-indian-school-records -1884-1980.htm.

Andrews, Evan. "When Native American Activists Occupied Alcatraz Island." History.com, November 20, 2023. (Updated July 11, 2023.) https://www.history.com/news /native-american-activists-occupy-alcatraz-island-45-years-ago.

Blecha, Peter. "Dover, Harriette Shelton Williams (1904–1991)." HistoryLink, essay 9079. July 27, 2009. https://www.historylink.org/File/9079.

Bohn, Terry. "Frank Jude." Society for American Baseball Research. https:// sabr.org/bioproj/person/Frank-Jude/.

Brando, Elizabeth. "Wilma Mankiller." National Women's History Museum. https://www.womenshistory.org/education-resources/biographies /wilma-mankiller.

Chemawa School, Bureau of Indian Education. "Chemawa Indian School: Chemawa History." 2015. https://chemawa.bie.edu/history.html.

Flood, Donna Jones. "American History: Chilocco School." *Electric Scotland*. https://electricscotland.com/history/america/donna/chilocco_school.htm.

History.com. "American Indian Movement (AIM)." October 31, 2022. (Updated September 28, 2023.) Accessed November 15, 2023. https://www.history.com/topics/native-american-history /american-indian-movement-aim.

History Matters: The U.S. Survey Course on the Web. "A Bill of Rights for the Indians: John Collier Envisions an Indian New Deal." https:// historymatters.gmu.edu/d/5059/.

———. "We Took Away Their Best Lands, Broke Treaties: John Collier Promised to Reform Indian Policy." https://historymatters.gmu.edu /d/5058.

Johnson, Dr. Troy. "We Hold the Rock: Alcatraz Indian Occupation." National Park Service. https://www.nps.gov/alca/learn/historyculture /we-hold-the-rock.htm.

Kershner, Jim. "Chief Joseph (1840–1904)." History Link, essay 8975. April 7, 2009. https://www.historylink.org/File/8975.

National Park Service. "The Carlisle Indian Industrial School: Assimilation with Education After the Indian Wars (Teaching with Historic Places)." Updated July 21, 2023. https://www.nps.gov/articles /the-carlisle-indian-industrial-school-assimilation-with-education -after-the-indian-wars-teaching-with-historic-places.htm.

National WWII Museum. "Second Lieutenant Ernest Childers Medal of Honor." November 4, 2020. https://www.nationalww2museum.org /war/articles/ernest-childers-medal-of-honor.

"1953: Congress Seeks to Abolish Tribes, Relocate American Indians." Native Voices: Native Peoples' Concepts of Health and Illness, NIH National Library of Medicine. https://www.nlm.nih.gov/nativevoices/timeline /488.html.

Rhodes, Eric. "Indian New Deal," Pieces of History, US National Archives. https://prologue.blogs.archives.gov/2015/11/30/indian-new-deal/.

Running Strong for American Indian Youth. "Drum and Song in Native American Cultures." https://indianyouth.org/drum-and -song-in-native-american-cultures/.

Women's History Matters. "Champions: The Girls of Fort Shaw." April 3, 2014. https://montanawomenshistory.org/champions/.

Federal Documents and Scholarly Papers

Annual Report of the Secretary of the Interior for the Fiscal Year ending June 30, 1890, vol. 2. Washington, DC: Government Printing Office, 1890.

Carlson, Kristen Matoy. "Bringing Congress and Indians Back into Federal Indian Law: The Restatement of the Law of American Indians." *Washington Law Review*, vol. 97, no. 3 (October 1, 2022). https:// digitalcommons.law.uw.edu/wlr/vol97/iss3/8/.

Chilocco Indian Agricultural School National Register of Historic Places Registration, US Department of the Interior, National Park Service. September 8, 2006. https://npgallery.nps.gov/GetAsset /c417f3db-f1d9-452c-8d2c-f6412e679200.

Dawes Act (General Allotment Act), Statutes at Large 24, 388-91, NADP Document A1887, February 8, 1887, US National Archives, Washington, DC. https://www.archives.gov/milestone-documents /dawes-act.

Haaland, Deb. "Statement of Deb Haaland, Secretary of the US Department of the Interior Before the Senate Committee on Indian Affairs." June 22, 2022. https://www.indian.senate.gov/hearings /oversight-hearing-volume-1-department-interior-s-federal-indian -boarding-school-initiative/.

Indian Child Welfare Act (ICWA), 25 U.S. Code Chapter 21, Tribal Law and Policy Institute. https://www.tribal-institute.org/lists/icwa.htm.

Indian Education: A National Tragedy—A National Challenge (The Kennedy Report): 1969 Report of the Committee on Labor and Public Welfare, US Senate, and Special Subcommittee on Indian Education. Washington, DC: Government Printing Office. https://files.eric .ed.gov/fulltext/ED034625.pdf.

Indian Reorganization Act (Act of June 18, 1934), Chapter 576 of the 73rd Congress, Approved June 18, 1934, as Amended May 12, 2006. https:// www.govinfo.gov/content/pkg/COMPS-5299/pdf/COMPS-5299.pdf.

Johnson, Rachael Renee. "The Navajo Special Program in the Pacific Northwest: Educating Navajo Students at Chemawa Indian Boarding School, 1946–1957." Thesis, Washington State University. August 2010. https://www.dissertations.wsu.edu/Thesis/Summer2010 /r_johnson_081310.pdf.

List of Federal Indian Boarding Schools, US Department of the Interior, April 1, 2022. https://www.bia.gov/sites/default/files/dup/inline-files /appendix_a_b_school_listing_profiles_508.pdf.

"Meriam Report: The Problem of Indian Administration (1928)." National Indian Law Library. https://narf.org/nill/resources/meriam.html.

Newland, Bryan. "Federal Indian Boarding School Initiative Investigative Report." Washington, DC: US Department of the Interior, Office of the Secretary. May 2022. https://www.bia.gov/sites/default/files/dup /inline-files /bsi_investigative_report_may_2022_508.pdf.

Proclamation No. 10285, 86 Fed. Reg. 57321 (October 8, 2021).

Ruckelshaus, William D. "EPA Policy for the Administration of Programs on Indian Reservations." November 8, 1984. https://www.epa.gov /tribal/epa-policy-administration-environmental-programs-indian -reservations-epa-indian-policy.

Starita, Joe. "Standing Bear's Courtroom Speech—Native American Heritage Month," excerpts from "The Case of Standing Bear: Establishing Personhood Under the Law." *Court Review*, vol. 45, no. 4 (2009). United States Courts. https://www.uscourts.gov /about-federal-courts/educational-resources/annual-observances /standing-bears-courtroom-speech-native.

Stewart, Kelly Leah. "(Re)writing and (Re)righting California Indian Histories: Legacies of St. Boniface Industrial School 1890 to 1935." Master of Arts Thesis, American Indian Studies, University of California Los Angeles. 2018. https://escholarship.org/uc/item/5qx1w2mz.

Termination: House Concurrent Resolution 108 (67 Stat. B132), Bureau of Indian Affairs Records, US National Archives. https://www.archives .gov/research/native-americans/bia/termination.

Warren, Elizabeth. "Truth and Healing Commission on American Indian Boarding School Policies in the US Act, S.1723," 118th Congress. May 15, 2023. https://www.warren.senate.gov/imo/media/doc/One %20Pager_118th.pdf.

Websites

American Indian Movement (AIM). https://www.aimovement.org/.

Carlisle Indian School Digital Resource Center, Archives & Special Collections. Waidner-Spahr Library, Dickinson College, Carlisle, PA. https://carlisleindian.dickinson.edu/.

Chilocco History Project (Research, Photographs, Interviews, Documentary, Educator Resources). https://chilocco.library.okstate.edu/.

Deaths at Chemawa Indian School, Pacific University Archives. https://
heritage.lib.pacificu.edu/s/deaths-chemawa/page/welcome.

Grace Thorpe Photographic Collection, Smithsonian National Museum of
the American Indian. https://sova.si.edu/record/NMAI.AC.085.

National Native American Boarding School Healing Coalition (NABS).
https://boardingschoolhealing.org/.

Native Languages of the Americas: Preserving and Promoting American
Indian Languages. http://www.native-languages.org/.

Ponca Tribe of Indians of Oklahoma. https://www.ponca-nsn.gov.

Curriculum

"The Experience of Native American Students in Boarding Schools, 19th
and 20th Centuries." Discovering Native Histories Along the
Lewis and Clark Trail, NEH Summer Institute, June 30–July 21,
2019. https://blogs.uoregon.edu/nativehistories/curriculum/authors
/the-experience-of-native-american-students-in-boarding-schools-19th
-and-20th-centuries/.

Prillaman, Barbara. "Indian Boarding Schools: A Case Study of
Assimilation, Resistance, and Resilience." Yale National Initiative to
Strengthen Teaching in Public Schools. https://teachers.yale.edu/
curriculum/viewer/initiative_16.01.09_u.

Interviews and Correspondence

Baker, Jim; oral history, *Chilocco History Project*, accessed October 19, 2023,
from https://chilocco.library.okstate.edu/items/show/2634.

Collins, Metha Gives Water; interview with Ponca Tribal members; October
23, 1969; shared 2023.

Jones, Denise; oral history, Chilocco History Project. https://chilocco.library
.okstate.edu/items/show/2637.

Lajimodiere, Denise K.; history of the National Native American Boarding
School Healing Coalition (N-NABS-HC), submitted to NABS board
members, February 2018.

Warrior, Della; email messages to Dan SaSuWeh Jones, June 21, 2023 and
July 7, 2023.

Videos

Oklahoma Oral History Program, Fire Thief Productions, Oklahoma State
University, and Chilocco National Alumni Association. "Chilocco
Through the Years (Broadcast Version)," August 2, 2019. https://www
.youtube.com/watch?v=LuQtljaCYzo.

ReactMedia.com. "Indigenous People React to Indigenous Representation in
Film and TV (Pocahantas, The Lone Ranger)," YouTube, October 14,
2019. https://www.youtube.com/watch?v=7ZkyL5pn74E.

University of Nebraska Medical Center. "Bitter Tears: Intergenerational
Trauma and American Indian Boarding Schools," Denise K.
Lajimodiere, December 12, 2022. https://www.unmc.edu/newsroom/2022/
12/12/author-shares-history-of-american-indian-boarding-schools/.

PHOTO CREDITS

ACKNOWLEDGMENTS

I wish to acknowledge all the American Indian children and their parents who experienced the boarding school era and the hundreds of thousands of their descendants. Bad or good, all boarding school experiences came with a price: the decimation of ancient tribal cultures and traditions. I wanted to capture a snapshot of that history, to give readers the opportunity to see my own family's experiences as well as other experiences across the nation, to better understand what it was like during the US government's hundred-year attack on American Indian culture.

Writing about one's own family can be problematic for any number of reasons, but suffice it to say, it's difficult. For one thing, people—even people who are close to you—can have differing memories of the same experience. To help navigate those discrepancies, Denise K. Lajimodiere, Turtle Mountain Band, Chippewa, was an invaluable member of the team, with her expertise and deep history of Indian education. I was excited that she came on board with us.

I wish to acknowledge all the descendants of the ancestor who opens this book, Little Moon There Are No Stars Tonight. Thank you to her children: Edward Pensoneau and my mother, Velma Pensoneau Jones; Edward and Velma's half brothers and sister Daniel Hernandez, Francis Poncho Hernandez, and Otilia Hernandez; and all their children who in our Ponca culture I call my brothers and sisters. You know who you are, and you know our relationship. I must acknowledge Michele Hernandez Hunt for supplying photos. I have a special book for you, my lovely niece, whose father I miss greatly. He was a major influence on me, and I looked up to him in so many ways (Thing Ga Ronnie). I must acknowledge the members of my own family, the children of Velma Louise Pensoneau Jones and Lee Otis Jones: Anthony Jones Rodriquez (a book in himself), Donna Colleen Jones Flood, Dennis Michael Jones, Alvin Lee Jones, and Esther Inez Jones Epperson.

I write this with a special recognition of my sister Donna Colleen Jones Flood, who shared her experiences at Chilocco Indian Agricultural School for the book. Donna lost her battle in life while we were completing this book. Donna was my mother at times, while our mother and father were busy making a life for us, and making ends meet. At least, sister, the pain and suffering are no longer a struggle for you (Thing Ga Sister).

I want to thank my sister Charmaine Pensoneau Baker and her husband, Jim Baker. All our conversations on this subject and the support they have given me over the years, especially while working on this book, cannot be overstated. The tireless work you both have been doing for the Chilocco National Alumni Association has not gone unnoticed. Sister, your beautiful poetry always says what most can only feel. Last, but never ever to be least, is our brother Steve Lanier Pensoneau. Our philosophical chats have lasted me a lifetime, maybe two. The volumes of literature you consume, especially on this subject, have fueled our conversations and kept me on my toes.

I can't thank enough those early members of my tribe, now passed away, for the stories that were handed down to me. And our current Chairman, Oliver Lewis Little Cook, for all the talks we've had about our family. We share a direct ancestor, our great-grandmother, Esther Broken Jaw Little Cook. Oliver's grandfather was David Little Cook, while my grandmother was Elizabeth Little Cook (Little Moon There Are No Stars Tonight). Oliver's father, Amos Little Cook, and my mother were brother and sister in the Ponca culture. I love my tribe and I love the people who make it my tribe. Of course, we have problems in our families just like any other families, but the Ponca system of relationships is good, and it works for the greater good of the Ponca. This acknowledgement of my tribe is very important to me.

I wish to acknowledge the Art Institute of Chicago for taking a back seat to this book in the artwork I'm creating for you. Covid was a major factor in delaying our contract, but thank you for keeping our project going and for your belief in me and my art abilities. It's coming next.

A special thanks to Della Warrior, who shared stories of her husband with me and corrected some misconceptions about her husband, Clyde Warrior. Your influence on Clyde was a major factor in the rise of his voice and his powerful mind. Your love for him was so important for our Ponca brother Clyde Warrior, a warrior far ahead of his time.

For Deb Haaland, Secretary of the Interior, for your voice and powerful hand in this important matter that has affected so many of us today. A truly Manly Hearted Woman you are, a warrior on the battlefield with tools and weapons to heal and change the hearts of men!

Finally, if not the best for last, certainly the most important. To my editor and collaborator Barbara Brownell Grogan, who convinced me to write this book. I assured Barbara I had no interest in writing a story about my family, especially our experience with the boarding school era. It's not part of my culture to put one's family above anyone else's family. But it was she who insisted that this was a story that needed to be told, that would help countless others who have suffered the experience or benefited from the shelter. A story that needed to be told but which had been buried. Barbara, thank you for picking me up off the floor and setting me back at my keyboard after so many falls while writing. Sometimes my eyes were so full of tears thinking of the horrors suffered by children that I couldn't see the screen to write at all! But it was you, Barbara, who helped me keep the faith in what we were doing. That my personal pain at the memories could be resolved by telling this story and that I could help the many who were suffering the same as my family, gave me hope. And to William Albea, the assistant editor who combed the manuscript to clarify terms and concepts, to ensure that young readers will fully appreciate this story. Will also led the photo research efforts, reaching into the Chilocco and Carlisle archives as well as other sources, to identify imagery to complement my family pictures. Kevin Mulroy, publisher at Potomac Global Media, was a strong support the entire way, believing in this project.

Thank you to Jody Corbett, my editor at Scholastic, for her laser-focused questions and deep insights that brought the manuscript to a higher level. Many thanks to Maeve Norton, Lisa Broderick, and Kassy Lopez, as well as to Emily Teresa and Cian O'Day, who really brought things together on the photo research. For Gregg Deal, whose cover art is both empowering and uplifting. Many thanks to the rest of the Scholastic team for their support and efforts: Lisa Sandell, David Levithan, Ellie Berger, Erin Berger, Seale Ballenger, Amanda Trautman, Rachel Feld, Katie Dutton, Corley Grayson, Lizette Serrano, Emily Heddleson, Maisha Johnson, Sabrina Montiengro, Meredith Wardell, Elizabeth Whiting, Jarad Waxman, Jody Stigliano, Jaquelin Rubin, Dan Moser, and the rest of the sales team.

ABOUT THE AUTHOR

Dan SaSuWeh Jones is the critically acclaimed author of *Living Ghosts & Mischievous Monsters: Chilling American Indian Stories* and was a storyteller and consultant for *National Geographic Encyclopedia of the American Indian*. A former Chairman of the Ponca Tribe of Indians of Oklahoma and a former member of the Producers Guild of America, he is also a filmmaker who has produced work for *Sesame Street*, NBC, TBS, and other national and international networks. He worked as an honorary Imagineer and consultant for the Walt Disney Company's Disney America theme park and as a field producer for the television miniseries *500 Nations*, produced by Kevin Costner. As a bronze sculptor, he was a finalist in the competition for the American Indian Veterans Memorial at the National Museum of the American Indian in Washington, DC. He holds a seat in the House of Warriors, a traditional Ponca Warrior Society.